LINKING ASSESSMENT TO READING COMPREHENSION INSTRUCTION

A FRAMEWORK FOR ACTIVELY ENGAGING LITERACY LEARNERS, K–8

Nora L. White
Texas Woman's University

Nancy L. Anderson
Texas Woman's University

Happy Carrico
Denton Independent School District

PEARSON

Boston   New York   San Francisco
Mexico City   Montreal   Toronto   London   Madrid   Munich   Paris
Hong Kong   Singapore   Tokyo   Cape Town   Sydney

Vice President and Executive Publisher: Jeffery W. Johnston
Senior Editor: Linda Ashe Bishop
Senior Managing Editor: Pamela D. Bennett
Senior Project Manager: Mary M. Irvin
Editorial Assistant: Demetrius Hall
Senior Art Director: Diane C. Lorenzo
Cover Design: Diane Y. Ernsberger
Operations Specialist: Laura Messerly
Director of Marketing: Quinn Perkson
Marketing Manager: Krista Clark
Marketing Coordinator: Brian Mounts

For related titles and support materials, visit our online catalog at www.pearsonhighered.com

Library of Congress Cataloging-in-Publication Data

White, Nora L.
   Linking assessment to reading comprehension instruction : a framework for actively engaging literacy learners, K–8 / Nora L. White, Nancy L. Anderson, Happy Carrico.
      p. cm.
   Includes bibliographical references.
   ISBN-13: 978-0-13-119127-3 (pbk.)
   ISBN-10: 0-13-119127-6 (pbk.)
   1. Reading comprehension.   2. Language arts—Ability testing.   3. Lesson planning.
I. Anderson, Nancy L., Ph. D.   II. Carrico, Happy.   III. Title.
LB1573.7.W48 2009
372.47—dc22

                                                              2008031943

Printed in the United States of America

10 9 8 7 6 5 4 3 2 1   [CIN]   12 11 10 09

PREFACE

Providing high-quality literacy instruction is one of the most important responsibilities of K–8 teachers. While the battle of confidence between teachers' abilities and test results rages on, expert teachers continue to make powerful moment-by-moment decisions that make all the difference in students' development. Expert teachers observe students every day and understand which behaviors are indicative of learning. They make decisions based on patterns of evidence of students' strengths and needs. Furthermore, expert teachers are critical consumers of the multitude of lessons that are readily available in published texts and on the Internet. The purpose of this book is to make visible to novice teachers the process that expert teachers engage in as they plan effective literacy lessons.

Our work with novice teachers has taught us that they need to *experience* quality literacy lessons as they begin to develop expertise in decision making. Novice teachers experience effective instruction when they have scaffolds for designing effective literacy lessons. Scaffolds for designing effective instruction must center on connecting assessment to instruction. Novice teachers are often told to connect instruction, but they are rarely shown or directly *experience* how to connect assessment to instruction.

With this need in mind, we developed an explicit framework for understanding how expert teachers connect student assessment to quality instruction in comprehension. Because understanding our assessment-to-instruction framework is understood best by example, our text also provides 20 model lessons that illustrate how to adapt instruction to meet students' strengths and needs. Each lesson follows a step-by-step process illustrating how to link assessment with instruction and makes the process explicit. These specific lessons can be used by all K–8 teachers who want to learn more about how to use students' strengths to extend their comprehension of text.

OUR RESEARCH BASE

Two areas of research particularly influenced this book: Dr. Marie Clay's writing and work in early literacy and ethnographic literature about language and literacy practices and how to apply these tools to the practice of effective observation. Underlying our framework of how to connect assessment with instruction is an orienting theory of teaching, learning, and reading comprehension that has been greatly informed by the work of Dr. Richard Allington. We build on his "thoughtful literacy" model in our development of 20 model lessons.

University instructors will find our book beneficial for a wide number of literacy education courses at the preservice and inservice level.

ACKNOWLEDGMENTS

The making of a first book involves an endless round of questioning, consulting, and revision. In our case, collaboration extended over 4 years. White and Anderson are indebted for a range of institutional supports and, more important, for encouragement from our Texas Woman's University/Department of Reading colleagues. Our Chair, Margaret Compton, supported and encouraged our work throughout the entire process. Carrico wishes to thank Denton Independent School District Superintendent Ray Braswell for encouragement and granting time from her regular schedule to participate in the development of this book.

We are grateful to the many teachers and university students for reading and providing feedback on our earlier drafts of the literacy lessons. Special thanks to Kristin Fulton, whose in-depth work with Karl is featured as an example in Part II. We are also grateful to the kindergarten–8th grade students for providing rich responses to the lessons taught. We would like to express our deepest gratitude to our editor, Linda Bishop, for the incredible level of support and encouragement during the development of this book. We are also very grateful to her assistant, Demetrius Hall, for his patience in accepting and organizing our many shipments and electronic transmissions of draft copies.

We thank the reviewers of our manuscript for their thoughtful comments and insights: Valerie Chapman, University of Texas at El Paso; Cindy Dooley, Western Illinois University; Margot Kinberg, National University; Priscillia Manarino-Leggett, Fayetteville State University; Debra Price, Sam Houston State University; Janet Richards, University of South Florida; and Barbara V. Senesac, Central Michigan University.

We also wish to thank Robert Tierney for his careful reading and thoughtful feedback and comments.

We are indebted to our families for putting up with the work of this book with encouragement and endless patience.

CONTENTS

Part I
Introduction

Through our experiences as teachers, administrators, and teacher educators, we have found that the link between assessment and instruction remains an abstract concept, talked about often, clearly visible in expert teachers' classrooms, but rarely demonstrated and made explicit. *Linking Assessment to Reading Comprehension Instruction* shows teachers how to link student assessment data with literacy instruction (International Reading Association, 2003; National Council of Teachers of English, 2004) specifically designed to support comprehension. This book provides an explicit framework for all teachers to learn how to teach comprehension literacy lessons effectively.

To effect learning, teachers must actively engage students in meaningful experience (Bruner, 1990; Lyons, 2003). Experience drives expertise (Wood, 1998). Novice teachers, as learners, need scaffolds to experience quality in order to develop expertise (Gambrell, Morrow, & Pressley, 2007; Lyons & Pinnell, 2001). The scaffolds in this book are explicit generative frameworks to help novice teachers learn how to link assessment to comprehension instruction. As they use the scaffolds, they will experience quality teaching and develop new levels of expertise. As a result, their students will become literate and achieve more in their classrooms.

Our book, organized in three parts, provides scaffolds to support teachers' developing expertise. We begin in Part I with the research and published theories of literacy and comprehension we use daily in our teaching and learning. Then we provide an explicit framework demonstrating how expert teachers can connect assessment to comprehension instruction. Finally, we make the processes visible and extend the scaffold by providing 20 literacy lessons we commonly use in primary- to middle-school classrooms.

Our adaptations of the lessons explicitly demonstrate how expert teachers connect instruction and assessment. Expert teachers know when to use a particular literacy lesson based on assessments and can explain *why* the lesson fits a particular student's strengths and needs. They know *what* the lesson will help students

TABLE I.1 Model Lesson Framework

WHAT
Summarizes *what* the lesson will teach students.
WHY
Explains *why* the instruction is needed to support students' comprehension strategies.
WHEN
Provides examples from student assessments showing competencies or needs, demonstrating *when* a lesson is appropriate for students.
HOW
Demonstrates *how* to teach with step-by-step directions.
WHO
Explains how to adapt lessons for various teaching routines—*who*—whole class, small group, one to one, including how to differentiate lessons for use with bilingual and English language learners (ELLs).

learn how to do and have a clear plan of *how* to implement the lesson. Finally, they understand how to adapt the lesson flexibly based on *who* is taking part in the lesson—an individual, small group, whole class, or a student whose first language is not English, or an English language learner (ELL).

To make the lessons accessible and easy to read, we have organized them according to how expert teachers think about connecting assessment to instruction, concisely illustrating the *what, why, when, how,* and *who* of teaching. We also provide examples of students' work across grade levels for many of the lessons. Table I.1 illustrates how the model lessons are organized according to how expert teachers think about teaching literacy comprehension.

LITERACY AND COMPREHENSION

To meet the needs of students, teachers need to reflect and identify their personal orienting theories of literacy teaching and learning. To model this process of reflection, we provide our orienting theory of literacy learning and connect this theory to our beliefs about teaching comprehension. These beliefs are grounded in the notion that we must shift instruction away from a focus on teaching students to read and recite known facts to more thoughtful literacy instruction (Allington, 2006).

LITERACY

Literacy learning is a complex process (Clay, 2001; Gee, 1989; Goodman, 1968, 1979). People of all ages and cultural backgrounds encounter and achieve many forms of literacy—for example, the varied literacies of family, media, computer, art, math, and numeracy. A vast body of research explores literacy as relevant practices rather than a simple product or set of isolated skills (Barton, 1994; Barton & Hamilton, 1998; Bloome & Green, 1991; Genishi, 1992; Gilmore, 1986; Lave, 1993; Morrow, 2003; Morrow, Gambrell, & Pressley, 2003; Pappas, Kiefer, & Levstik, 1999; Taylor, 1983; Wells & Claxton, 2002). What marks a person as literate is related to what forms of literacy practices occur in particular social situations—how literacy is used in different situations and settings (Freire & Macedo, 1987; Gee, 2005; B. Street, 1994; Tierney & Rogers, 1986; Tuyay, Floriani, Yeager, Dixon, & Green, 1995). The main goal of school literacy instruction should be to support students in gaining access and success in literacy-based social interactions, marking them as literate in the real world.

School-based literacy instruction is more effective when teachers make learning relevant. By *relevant*, we mean having a bearing on or importance in students' lives—their language, culture, family, friends, needs, and interests. Too often, curriculum takes little account of what individual students bring to the lesson, failing to connect with the student's innate capacity to make sense of the world. By connecting assessment to instruction in a systemic way, through careful observation, teachers craft relevant and more effective teaching.

Recognizing and placing value on many literacy practices supports students' abilities to access the literacies that surround their daily lives. To place value on multiple literacies, teachers must first consider their personal theories of literacy (Street & Street, 1991; Taylor, Coughlin, & Marasco, 1997; Weaver, 2002). There are three major reasons why this is a critical task:

1. Teachers' practical knowledge, made up of personal systems of beliefs and principles, influence teaching actions (Elbaz, 1981).
2. Making theories explicit allows for constant comparison, helping us deal with dissonance and subsequent shifts in our understandings.
3. Teachers who articulate the "what and why," or theory of their practice, successfully challenge ineffective policy mandates and "one-size-fits-all" practices, thus advocating for all students' unique developmental paths (Lyons, 2003)

One-dimensional, simple theories of reading or writing as the sum of skill sets mastered and tested are inadequate for describing the complexities of school-based literacy learning (Clay, 1998; Paratore & McCormack, 2007; Routman, 1996). Becoming literate means students construct literate identities at school and home (Gee, 2005) while assembling the complex processing systems necessary to construct meaning from written language (Clay, 2001; Goodman, 1996). To be literate, students must learn how to engage in the practices of being literate—how to understand rather than recite known facts and how to talk with others about texts read. The assessments in this book guide teachers to *begin* to understand the complexities involved in literacy learning, particularly comprehension.

COMPREHENSION

Comprehension has been defined in complex ways, and myriad typologies, strategies, or skills may be found in the professional literature. We build on the work of the RAND Study Group's (Snow, Science and Technology Policy Institute [Rand

Corporation], & U.S. Office of Educational Research and Improvement, 2002) extensive review of comprehension research and explain how the book relates to the major research findings.

The RAND Study Group's review of research related to comprehension asserts that comprehension cannot be separated from a sociocultural context where learners construct identities. Embedded in the sociocultural context are three critical comprehension elements: the *reader*, the *text*, and the *activity*. What follows is an explanation of how this book deals with each of these elements.

The Reader   Elements related to the reader mean who is doing the comprehending. Teachers see overt signs of reader-based factors by carefully listening and attentively observing when assessing students. The assessment framework in this book guides teachers to examine reader-based factors or a student's unique ways of constructing meaning.

The Text   Text elements include the text that is to be comprehended. In this book, we connect reading and writing as intertwined message-construction and production-processing systems. Thus the text-based factors in the literacy lessons are influenced by the particular lessons and texts the teacher selects. Text-based factors are critical to comprehension; however, an in-depth analysis of genre and text structures is beyond the scope of this book.

The Activity   Activity elements are critical factors. What students do, or the activity involved in teaching, influences comprehension. For example, a student may be able to provide a thoughtful summary of a book to a friend when recommending it but may miss a "summary" question on a multiple-choice test. The 20 lessons provided in this book make explicit the ways to engage in literate activity with students—not only individuals, but small groups, whole classes, and bilingual students.

THOUGHTFUL LITERACY

Because comprehension is defined in complex ways and influenced by readers, texts, and activities, we need thinking tools to help us examine our theory and link assessments to instruction. The basis for the thinking tool related to comprehension in this book is Richard Allington's (2006) description of "thoughtful literacy." Thinking tools begin with a guiding theory. This book draws on thoughtful literacy and offers support and guidance to scaffold thinking in the form of charts, figures, or questions. Through repeated use, or experience, the frameworks become part of teachers' examinations of personal theories; the frameworks transform the teachers' decision-making system. As expertise develops, the frameworks are no longer necessary.

We need thinking tools related to comprehension instruction because recitation and recall of correct answers as measured by multiple-choice questions of contrived testing texts permeates schools in the United States (Meier, 2002). Through test preparation, students read contrived text written for the sole purpose of testing for understanding. As a result, teachers unknowingly simplify comprehension through teaching for answers to questions as opposed to thinking about text. Students who struggle with literacy learning are at an even greater risk of teaching that is reduced to interrogations for the right answer. Allington (2006) asserts, "Outside of school settings we engage in conversations about the adequacy of text and authors to inform, engage and entertain us; in school we engage in interrogations around what was in the text" (p. 111).

How can we begin to move away from unknowingly interrogating students? In this book, thoughtful literacy refers to making sense of texts in ways that represent being literate in social interactions inside and outside of school. Essentially, teaching for thoughtful literacy means teaching students to think in ways that go beyond completing a task, to how the task will help students make sense of text outside of school. Jerome Bruner (1973; Bruner & Weinreich-Haste, 1987) first proposed this concept in his research that showed how children will "go beyond the information given." Students are born with the innate ability to move beyond what is presented to them, and relevant school-based literacy instruction harnesses this powerful innate process (Bruner, 1973). This is the essential question to ask when planning instruction to help students move beyond the information and teach for thoughtful literacy: "Is what I'm saying or doing going to help the child be successful with this text as well as new texts he or she encounters in and out of school?"

The literacy lessons in this book emphasize thoughtful literacy. However, the lessons may also be taught in ways that reflect comprehension as outcomes and answers. The decision-making process unique to each teacher determines the

Figure I.1 Thoughtful Literacy Connections

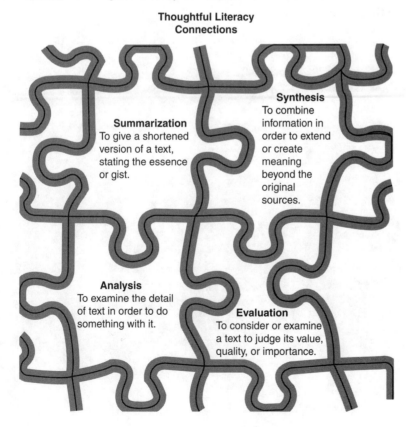

Thoughtful Literacy Connections

Summarization
To give a shortened version of a text, stating the essence or gist.

Synthesis
To combine information in order to extend or create meaning beyond the original sources.

Analysis
To examine the detail of text in order to do something with it.

Evaluation
To consider or examine a text to judge its value, quality, or importance.

emphasis. For example, teachers may use "learning logs" (a method of taking notes while reading, presented in Lesson 7) as a way to record information to complete a book report for an assignment. In this context, learning logs represent remembering facts so as to be successful with literacy in school. Conversely, a learning log may be relevant to students' subsequent encounters with text when it is used as a means of interacting with and clarifying the important ideas in a text though writing. Teaching students to use learning logs in this way helps them interact and connect with texts in ways that help us move beyond the facts to make meaningful connections or be thoughtfully literate.

The notion of thoughtful literacy maintains complexity but is concise enough for teachers to use as a thinking tool. We have adapted Allington's framework into a thinking tool for both teaching and learning. We find many classrooms where emphasis is placed on teaching for authentic connections among texts, self, and world (Keene & Zimmerman, 2007). However, thoughtful literacy means the reader is "able to talk in certain ways that go beyond simply making connections" (Allington, 2006, p.113). The ways of talking about the connections reveal a complex, intertwined system of authentically summarizing, analyzing, synthesizing, and evaluating.

Although many school-based literacy tasks teach these thinking processes in isolation, in the real world they occur in a simultaneous process of connecting that leads to making sense of text. We consciously use the term *making sense of text* because we think thoughtful literacy applies to reading as well as writing. Figure I.1 illustrates how the thinking process connects together in a metaphorical puzzle. Each student constructs a puzzle in a unique way, determined by the activity, the task, and the reader.

Part II
Literacy Learning and Assessment of Comprehension

Deciding how and what to teach in the classroom can be difficult. A plethora of literacy assessment tools exists, all representing differing perspectives of literacy and comprehension development. Available sources include state-level standards, curriculum guides, published basal reading programs, and thematic units carefully crafted from content curriculum expectations. Although these sources may provide abundant resources—for example, outlines with objectives and activities—a key element may be missing: assessment of students' literacy understandings.

Thoughtful literacy comprehension is primarily a process of inquiry and interpretation, rather than recitation and memorization of known facts from texts. When students are engaged in thoughtful literacy practices, they are engaged in processes of understanding the meaning of their texts, the processes they engaged in while constructing an understanding, and, ultimately, what it means to comprehend—the difference that it makes in their daily lives.

By assessment, we do not mean testing. *Assess* comes from the Latin word *assidere*, meaning "to sit beside." Assessment is the process of closely observing and systematically interpreting observations in ways that tell us "what" to teach. Such an approach is much more useful than relying solely on published curriculum materials and assessments.

Through assessment, we uncover students' competencies and confusions. Analysis of students' strengths and needs fuels teaching decisions targeted toward specific learning outcomes. Because those targeted learning outcomes match a student's unique path to literacy, our instruction is more effective. The cornerstone of effective instructional planning is assessment.

Our goal here is to provide a comfortable starting point for beginning the process of linking assessment and instruction. We begin by asking key assessment questions that make up an explicit framework without oversimplifying this complex process. The following key questions can guide the process of linking assessment and instructional decision making:

- What dimension of "literacy learning" are we observing?
- How do we observe it?
- How do we analyze the information we collect?
- How do we plan instruction using this information?

Often we focus on one of these questions, neglecting the other concepts. For example, many comprehension-assessment tools are available. We could learn how to administer 10 tools but never learn how to analyze the information to plan day-to-day instruction. To scaffold teachers' decision making, we explain how observation is the cornerstone of effective assessment. Four dimensions of assessment support informed teaching decisions around comprehension:

- Conversations and inventories
- Observations of oral reading
- Observations of constructing and composing
- Responding to texts and comprehending: analysis, synthesis, summarizing, and evaluating

Observation: The Cornerstone of Assessment

Effective teachers observe and constantly formulate and reformulate beliefs about students. Judgments of what they think is happening are suspended until they have evidence to support interpretations. An ethnographic lens provides helpful tools for teachers to learn how to observe students more effectively.

Ethnography is the study of culture and how humans construct understandings of the world (Geertz, 2000; Green & Wallat, 1981; Marcus, 1998; Spindler, 1997; Wolcott, 1999). As human beings, we are always using filters to make sense of the world around us. These filters are constructed by our unique and individual prior experiences, which are shaped by our language, culture, family, friends, work, play, neighbors, communities, and so on (Bloome, 1982; Egan-Robertson & Bloome, 1998; Gee, 1999; Gumperz & Hymes, 1986; Langer, 1987; Lankshear, 1997; Schieffelin & Gilmore, 1986; Spindler, 1997; Zou & Trueba, 2002). Filtering is an important process of meaning making. We see, we connect, we understand.

A challenge for teachers is to find ways of exploring the connections and meanings of our students without being blinded by our own connections and meanings. The interpretations we make about what we observe are influenced by our point of view. An ethnographic perspective provides a lens to understand the patterns of student behavior that often become invisible because the behavior we observe seems regular and ordinary unless we develop strategies for making the invisible visible, the usual, strange.

The following example illustrates the notion of suspending judgment or interpretation until we have evidence of patterns of behaviors observed. We are taught from an early age that it is important to react, not hesitate, when we hear a fire alarm. We learn to exit a building when an alarm sounds, not to search for additional evidence to support the assumption that our lives might be at risk. People young and old understand that we should *not* say to ourselves, "I hear the alarm but I don't smell smoke or see flames. I think that I should wait until I know more.

FIGURE II.1 Learning to Observe

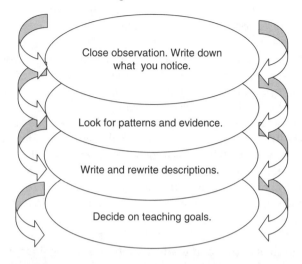

Perhaps the alarm went off by mistake. This has happened many times, and we have never had a fire in the building. I shouldn't jump to conclusions. I'll just wait."

Of course, this response to the fire alarm sounding makes little sense. If the majority of teachers and students responded with such hesitancy, disbelief, or skepticism, fire safety personnel would be outraged. Fire safety experts have systematically developed and implemented educational programs to teach people to respond without reflection or further evidence: We are taught to walk quickly and calmly out of the building to safety. There are times in our lives when it is important to make quick decisions based on limited patterns of evidence. Teaching literacy is not one of those times.

When we observe students, such hesitancy is critical to making the most effective interpretations. We need to remind ourselves *not* to jump to conclusions—*not* to respond as though the fire alarm sounded—when we observe students and interpret what is happening. We need to consider these questions: What are the patterns of students' responses? What do I notice? What do I think is happening? What is the evidence?

Expert teachers base interpretations on patterns of evidence by gathering multiple sources of observation data. Teachers learn how to make descriptive rather than interpretative statements until they have evidence-supporting conclusions. Such an approach helps us learn how to respond to students' strengths and needs—to see through their perspective—not ours.

Figure II.I illustrates how to begin observations using an ethnographic lens while assessing students' learning. An example is provided later in the chapter of how one teacher, Kristin, made use of observation as she planned instruction.

DIMENSIONS OF COMPREHENSION ASSESSMENT

Conversations and Inventories

When we really listen to students, we can hear their perspectives—how they make sense of their environment. Our responses to their perspectives must authentically communicate that they have something important to contribute to the classroom culture. Through conversations, we can understand how students make sense of their environment. From this understanding, we can construct responses that help students build connections to the meanings of their lives.

How Do We Observe Using Conversations and Inventories?   Conversations can be a form of assessment, especially when we take the time to record students' comments and our interpretations. To do this, sit with a student and create a purpose for talking (reading a book, sharing a picture, sharing a meaningful artifact). During that conversation, resist asking questions that result in one- or two-word or yes/no responses. Instead, use verbal and nonverbal signals to encourage elaborate responses from the student. When teachers become fascinated listeners, they experience real conversations with students. At the end of these conversations, take note of the content of the conversation and consider what the student revealed about his or her understandings and attitudes about literacy and the world around him or her.

Another tool that can uncover students' understanding is inventories. There are many types of inventories, such as lists of questions or responses to pictures, interest and attitude surveys, and reading strategy and cognitive inventories.

The strengths of surveys and checklist-formatted inventories are that they provide a list of questions to support teachers in gathering data on individual students and groups that show change over time in consistent, measurable ways. The weaknesses of inventories are that teachers control the direction and focus of the conversation. Through our control, we may turn a survey or checklist into an inquisition and lose the opportunity to uncover the complexities of students' worlds.

Oral Reading

Expert teachers sit beside each student and systematically observe reading to formulate supportive instruction that addresses individual literacy needs. The oral reading of novice and proficient readers makes decision making visible, supplying teachers with valuable information. Research on oral reading and self-correction of early readers suggests that the process of hearing what is read provides a feedback system that contributes to the development of processing systems. Because learning is a complex, constructive process, the overt decision making of the young child during oral reading becomes the internalized processing system of the older, proficient reader.

The complexity of how students' decision making changes over time may be described as "possible progressions in acts of processing" (Clay, 2001). When reading, students constantly search for information from print, their world, and what they know about problem solving from previous reading and writing experiences. As they search for meanings in text, students self-correct errors through a constant monitoring process of checking on the message construction (reading) or production (writing). Phrased and fluent reading is the outward sign or act of a successful processing system.

How Do We Observe Oral Reading?   During oral reading observations, specific tools focus our attention on key aspects of literacy development. The tools help us observe and record neutrally and systematically what we see, letting go of our assumptions. Three tools found in many classrooms for oral reading observations are running records (Clay, 2000), miscue analysis (Goodman, 1969, 1973; Goodman,

Goodman, & Hood, 1989), and published reading inventories (Beaver & Carter, 2006; Strickland & Strickland, 2000; Tierney & Readence, 2000). Each tool varies in complexity and the amount of training and expertise required for reliable use.

The tools are similar in use and focus. All three include the teacher sitting next to the student and observing while using a notation system to record oral reading. The analysis system for each tool includes a method for identifying whether the text was too hard, too easy, or instructionally appropriate. Errors in each tool are analyzed to understand how students make use of sources of information in text. For example, if a student read, "I ran to my home" for "I ran to my house," the miscue or error "home" for "house" would be analyzed. All three tools would point to the fact that the error has maintained the meaning of text while the letters and/or clusters look similar, indicating the use of grapho-phonic information. Readers will learn how to record and analyze students' oral reading using these tools.

Constructing and Composing

Students' writing is a gold mine of information about how they make sense of and make use of written language. Writing makes visible their linguistic pool of understanding almost as if it is displayed on a television screen (Clay, 1979). Students' hypothesis of how written language works is also revealed. Furthermore, how students view themselves as writers and represent their social worlds (Dyson, 1993; Rowe, 1994) provides powerful information about how they are constructing a literate identity.

Consider the complexity of what students do when they write. Students use their knowledge of the writing task at hand (for example, a written assignment, note to friend, or journal or diary entry), their world, and how to put letters and words together while honoring concepts about print to communicate an intended message. All of this must be done while simultaneously monitoring the intended message and self-correcting when necessary.

How Do We Observe Composing and Constructing? To generate a writing sample, refer to the previous section on how to generate a conversation with students. One way is to invite students openly to write about whatever they like. Because you are attempting to assess what they can do independently, if they appeal for help, simply turn the effort back to them and say, "You try it" or "You get to decide." As they write, take notes about how they verbalize their thinking processes. Be careful to keep your notes to what students *can* do as opposed to searching for weaknesses or making assumptions too quickly about ability.

Responding to Texts and Comprehending

The conversations and connections representing thoughtful literacy made while reading and writing texts are complex, unique, and do not occur in isolation. As we discussed in Part I, analysis, synthesis, summary, and evaluation of texts are interwoven and connected responses to reading and writing. The following ways of connecting to text frame the assessment tools described in this section:

Summarization: To give a shortened version of a text, stating the essence or gist.
Analysis: To examine the detail of text to do something with it.

Synthesis: To combine information to extend or create meaning beyond the original sources.

Evaluation: To consider or examine a text to judge its value, quality, or importance.

This is a key question: How can teachers observe and evaluate a student's understanding of a text in ways that support instruction that benefits a student's immediate needs? To do this, teachers need tools that provide opportunities for multiple responses from students.

How Do We Observe Responses to Text and Comprehending? Research has generated categories of the ways students comprehend. Instead of creating a list of "reading strategies," we feel it is important to understand students' perspectives and observe in ways that capture the unique ways students make sense. If we use a list, we focus our attention on specific aspects and may not notice an important response or we may see a diverse response as "wrong."

First, we propose engaging in a conversation about the book with students or responding to texts. Ask open-ended questions like "*What do you think about . . .*" and "*I'm wondering*" while avoiding yes/no questions or questions that simply ask for recall. Each of these questions can be addressed in a conversation or drawing. The goal is to draw as much out of the student as possible while having a genuine conversation about the text. This serves two very important purposes. You begin to understand how the student comprehended the book and you communicate to the student that his or her thinking counts and is worthy of your attention.

After the conversation, take careful notes about the student's responses and add them to your ongoing collection of data regarding the student. Some helpful ways of thinking about their responses are how they make inferences, evaluate, and extend the meanings in the text. If a student simply recalls details, perhaps he or she has been led to believe that talk about books has to do with getting the right answer to the teacher's questions.

The second tool is retelling—written, oral, or artistic. Retelling is not only an assessment tool but also an instructional strategy that helps students take greater control of text structures while making connections using their background knowledge. Using retelling as an assessment tool is appealing because it is suitable for a wide range of students, flexible, and relatively easy to prepare. Retelling can be useful but overused if we expect all students to retell text in the same manner. Try to place retelling in an authentic context. For example, ask the student to explain, write, or draw what this book is about to someone who has not read it.

An important feature of retelling is that students must understand the task and have clear demonstrations of what is expected, especially if a specific rubric is used to score their response. In this book we view retelling as a specific assessment or instructional method embedded in what it means to be literate in school settings. In other words, rarely in the world outside of school do we provide summaries keyed to specific rubrics for the texts we read.

Table II.1 provides an overview of how to link the four dimensions of assessment described above with tools for observing and assessing the student's comprehension of texts. Then, we introduce and discuss a useful assessment rubric to support ways of thinking about each dimension of assessment and to understand the data gathered through use of the tools and observations of the student's comprehension of texts read.

TABLE II.1   Overview of Assessment Tools Related to Comprehension

Dimensions of Assessment	Tools/Observations	Comprehending
Conversations/Inventories	⇒ Conversations ⇒ Surveys/Checklists	⇒ Attitudes ⇒ Interests
Oral Reading	⇒ Running records ⇒ Miscue analysis ⇒ Informal reading inventory	⇒ Decision making ⇒ Processing system ⇒ Phrasing and fluency
Composing and Constructing	⇒ Writing samples	⇒ Negotiating messages through text ⇒ Problem solving ⇒ Knowledge of letters and/or word patterns
Responding to Text	⇒ Conversations ⇒ Retelling ⇒ Oral and written responses to open-ended activities	⇒ Analysis ⇒ Synthesis ⇒ Summarizing ⇒ Evaluating

ASSESSMENT RUBRIC

The rubric in Table II.1 provides a very broad way of thinking about each assessment tool and how to analyze the data to understand more about the student's comprehension of texts. The rubric is organized according to the four dimensions of the assessment areas described previously. The levels of sophistication relate to instruction. In other words, where a child falls on the rubric indicates the type of instruction that would be most beneficial. The example in Table II.2 demonstrates the use of the rubric for assessment and planning instruction. Each literacy lesson described in this book links back to the assessment tools we have outlined.

ANALYZING ASSESSMENTS

In previous sections, the first two questions related to connecting assessment to instruction were explained. What aspect of literacy are we observing and how do we observe it? In this section, we discuss the next two questions: How do I analyze the information, and how do I plan instruction using the information? The examples of individual students may be adapted for small groups or whole class decision making.

How to Analyze the Assessments

To demonstrate how to analyze the assessment data, consider the example of Kristen, a first-year teacher, and Karl, a child who just completed first grade. Table II.3 describes Kristin's analysis of Karl's assessments. Kristin administered assessments related to letters, words, phonics, and concepts about print. Because the focus of the book is on comprehension, we only include the assessments related to comprehension. We explain each step Kristin used and provide examples in Table II.3.

> **STEP 1:**   *Look at the assessments.* Spread the assessment out on a large surface and visually scan the notes taken. Connect the information across assessments (see Table II.1).

TABLE II.2 Rubric for Analyzing Assessment Data

	Developing and Instructionally Dependent	On the Way to Independence	Independent and Needs More Challenge
Conversations and Inventories	• *Seldom* makes positive comments about the use of literacy in life. • Often makes negative comments about perceived reading/writing competence. • *Seldom* talks about books/writing. • *Rarely* initiates self-selection of books and reads. • *Rarely* writes about personal interests. • *Rarely* perceives reading/writing as enjoyable literacy events.	• *Sometimes* makes positive comments about the use of literacy in life. • *Sometimes* makes positive comments about perceived reading/writing competence. • *Sometimes* talks about books/writing. • *Sometimes* initiates self-selection of books and reads. • *Sometimes* writes about personal interests. • Perceives reading/writing as enjoyable literacy events.	• *Frequently* makes positive comments about the use of literacy in life. • *Consistently* makes positive comments about perceived reading/writing competence. • *Frequently* talks about books/writing. • *Frequently* initiates self-selection of books and reads. • *Frequently* writes about personal interests. • *Consistently* perceives reading/writing as enjoyable literacy events.
Oral Reading	• *Often* invents text; searches for predictable patterns in meaning, language structure. • *Searches* exclusively for letter/sound relationships at every point of difficulty. • *Infrequently* monitors and self-corrects. • *Rarely* reads at an instructional level of accuracy. • *Rarely* reads in a phrased and fluent manner; reads slow and word by word.	• *Often* integrates meaning, language structure, and grapho-phonic information. • *Sometimes* searches for different sources of information. • *Sometimes* monitors and self-corrects. • *Usually* reads at an instructional level of accuracy. • *Usually* reads phrased and fluent, slowing down and speeding up.	• *Consistently* integrates meaning, language structure, and grapho-phonic information. • *Flexibly* searches for different sources of information. • *Consistently* monitors and self-corrects. • *Consistently* reads at an instructional and easy level of accuracy. • *Consistently* reads in a phrased and fluent manner.
Constructing and Composing	• Oral and/or written language *rarely* evidence negotiation of intended message. • *Seems hesitant* to initiate problem solving of ways to record a message. • Knowledge of letters and/or patterns in words *is emerging*.	• Oral and/or written language *sometimes* evidence negotiation of intended message. • *Initiates some* problem solving to record a message. • Knowledge of letters and/or patterns in words *seems to be in construction*.	• Oral and/or written language *consistently* evidence negotiation of intended message. • *Initiates flexible* problem solving to record a message. • Knowledge of letters and/or patterns in words *is clear*.
Responding to Text and Comprehending: Summarizing	• *Seldom* reflects the gist of the author's intended message. • *Limited* information included in response.	• *Often* makes sense to the child but seldom reflects the gist of the author's message. • *Relevant* important information included in response.	• *Consistently* reflects the gist of the author's intended message. • *Significant* information included in response.

(continued)

TABLE II.2 Continued

	Developing and Instructionally Dependent	On the Way to Independence	Independent and Needs More Challenge
Responding to Text and Comprehending: Analyzing	• *Seldom* determines critical features of story structures in fiction (e.g., characters, setting, plot) and expository text structures in nonfiction (description, sequence, cause/effect). • *Unimportant* features of text emphasized.	• *Sometimes* determines critical features of story structures in fiction (e.g., characters, setting, plot) and expository text structures in nonfiction (description, sequence, cause/effect). • *Some* relevant features of text emphasized.	• *Consistently* determines critical features of story structures in fiction (e.g., characters, setting, plot) and expository text structures in nonfiction (description, sequence, cause/effect). • *Critical* features of the text emphasized.
Responding to Text and Comprehending: Synthesizing	• *Rarely* combines/connects multiple sources of information in a coherent fashion. • *Rarely* draws conclusions based on pertinent information. • Pulls together *irrelevant* information.	• *Sometimes* combines/connects multiple sources of information in coherent fashion. • *Sometimes* draws conclusions based on pertinent information in a coherent fashion • Pulls together *some relevant* information.	• *Consistently* combines/connects multiple sources of information in a coherent fashion. • *Sometimes* draws conclusions based on pertinent information in a coherent fashion. • Pulls together *very relevant* information.
Responding to Text and Comprehending: Evaluating	• *Rarely* takes a critical stance toward the text. • *Seldom and/or inappropriately* judges the quality of information available in order to make inferences.	• *Often* takes a critical stance toward the text. • *Often* and/or appropriately judges the quality of information available in order to make inferences.	• *Consistently* takes a critical stance toward the text. • *Consistently* and/or appropriately judges the quality of information available in order to make inferences.

STEP 2: *What did I notice?* Read all of your notes. Write down what you noticed with this question in mind: What do these data reveal about how the student makes sense of written language? Be specific, but suspend judgments or interpretations. In fact, the more specific you are, the more you will be able to see the effectiveness of your instruction. Try to avoid negative and deficit thinking while addressing areas of need. Move back and forward, adding to sections. For example, in Karl's analysis, Kristin connected composing and constructing with the written response. She also noted how his interest inventory connected to reading and writing responses. (See "What I Notice" in Table II.3).

STEP 3: *Analyze the assessment data.* After taking notes, the next step is to interpret them and draw conclusions about what you see. Write this down. (See the "Analysis: Possible Patterns" in Table II.3.) As you develop conceptual knowledge over time, what you see in the assessments will change. There is no right set of things to write. Rather, approach the writing tentatively, ready to be surprised and continually learn from your observations.

STEP 4: *Apply the rubric.* Look at the rubric. Using your notes and analysis, locate the criteria and column that best fits the child's present processing. Circle or highlight the criteria. In the chart provided in Table II.4, each

TABLE II.3 Kristin Analyzes Karl's Assessment

Conversations and Inventories

Literacy Identity & Interests

Literacy Interview & Attitude Survey

Do you like to read? What are you reading right now?

Sometimes - I like to color + play a lot. Transformers + Star Wars - I know a lot o their names - watched them. I bought toys @ Supertarge. Lizards - making a book on favorite pictures

How did you learn how to read?

practiced reading

When you are reading and you come to something that you don't know, what do you do? Do you ever do anything else?

Skip over word ; no

when he grows up
Dad's gone
to teach him
get a lizard
ninja

What does it mean to read? What does reading mean to you?

Saying words in a book - if he knows

What do you do when you don't understand something that you've read? Do you ever do anything else?

I say "I don't know that word", "use blends"

Learn about penguins

What would you do to help someone that is having trouble reading?

Do you like to write?

yes - what happened in a book - I copy out o a book, made pictures in a book

What would you like to do better as a reader?
how they made the book

make a book
1° all the pictures
. then put the words

What does it mean to write? What does writing mean to you?

its almost like drawing, how is it different from draw- making pictures write- make words

What would you like to do better as a writer?

writing - not sure word
"put an x"

My Favorite Things Inventory

When school is out each day, I like to:
write

When I'm on school vacation, my favorite things to do are:
"look at the house"

If I could do anything in the whole world, I would:
- I don't know

If I could read about anything I wanted, it would be:
boy going to his house

When I'm in school, my favorite things to do are:
Write in journals

My favorite hobbies are:
-

My favorite animals are:
lions

First grade:
free time - blocks

Chapter Books
. Bionacles

Chapter Books
- Milkweed
- All the books that I like

What I Notice

Sometimes likes to read; likes to color and play transformers.

Reading is saying words in a book—if he knows the word. If he doesn't know the word, he says, "I don't know that word."

Shifts topic to Dad and Iguana when asked about reading.

Writing, "I copy out of books."

He likes to write in journal but also says he copies words out of a book.

Analysis: Possible Patterns

Are reading and writing for meaning? POSSIBLE PATTERN? Reading is saying words in books and writing is copying words?

Seems to have at least one way of problem solving—copying. Glimmers of positive remarks because he likes to write in journals, but he seems to think writing is copying.

(continued)

16

TABLE II.3 Continued

Oral Reading

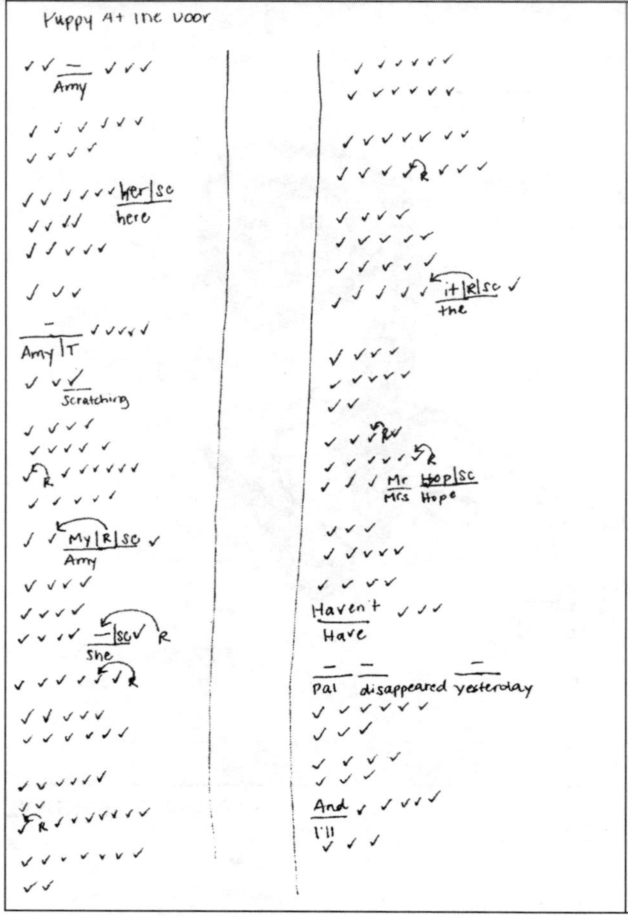

Puppy At The Door

(handwritten miscue analysis markings)

Amy / T
scratching

My|R|SC — Amy

— |&v|R She

Kit|R|SC the

Mr Hop|SC Mrs hvp°

Haven't — Have

— — Pal disappeared yesterday

And / I'll

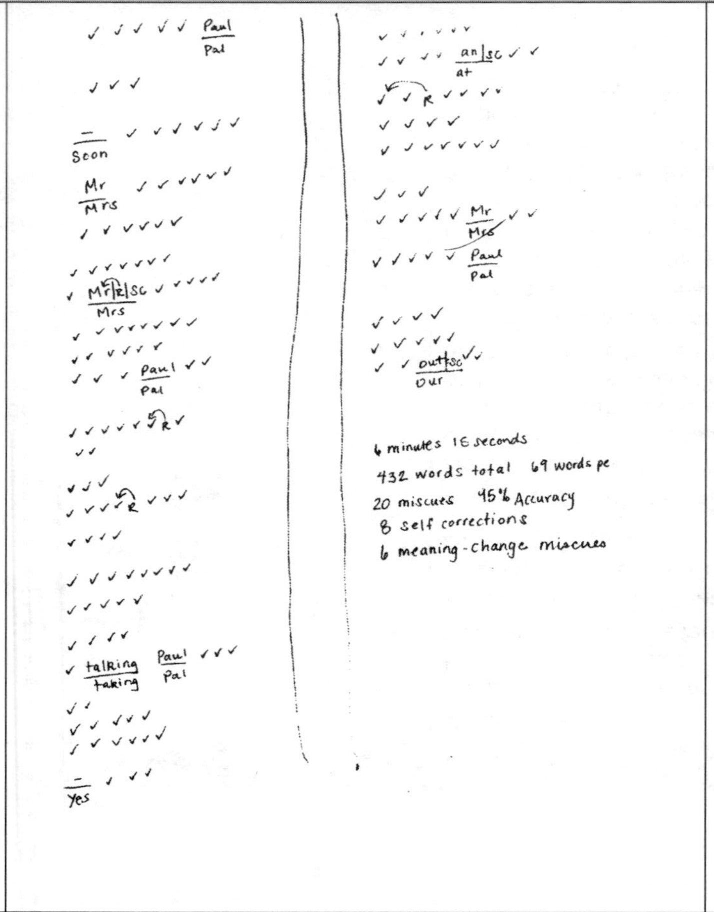

Paul Pal

— scon

Mr Mrs

M|R|SC Mrs

Paul Pal

talking taking

Paul Pal

— Yes

an|sc at

Mr Mrs

Paul Pal

out|sc our

6 minutes 16 seconds   69 words pr

432 words total   95% Accuracy

20 miscues

8 self corrections

6 meaning-change miscues

What I Notice

Continuous and smooth

Read with expression

20 miscues and 8 self-corrections

Six meaning-changing miscues

69 words per minute

Phrases fluent sounding

Analysis: Possible Patterns

Consistently integrates meaning and language structures with grapho-phonic information. Karl sometimes self-corrects. The text is instructional at 95% accuracy. Self-corrections show Karl monitors for meaning and searches in different ways. He rereads and appeals for help. He was also reading in a phrased and fluent manner. His errors seem to fit with the first part of a word and are meaningful while fitting structure.

(continued)

TABLE II.3 Continued

Oral Reading

Writing

What I notice

When invited to write about anything he wanted, Karl first drew a picture without talking. He then wrote letter and number-like forms from left to right.

When he was asked what he was drawing and writing, he said, "That's a King Cobra and that's my name in cursive and Egyptian."

Analysis: Possible Patterns

He drew a picture for composing. He didn't seem to overtly negotiate a message in his interest inventory; he indicated writing was copying words, so possible patterns may be he didn't write any word because there were none to copy.

Evidence in later response shows a pattern. When asked to respond to what he wrote, shows he can record using letters and words with a system in construction related to spelling patterns (spelling of animal).

He is thinking flexibly about how his name looks as a writer and is instructionally dependent. This is evidenced by the need for support to produce written responses.

(continued)

TABLE II.3 Continued

Karl

It's the kind
It's an anamale

There are endsoazs
there are caricters
there are words
obe ewon-kono boy

Notes on Written Response:

I asked him to tell me about his drawing and the cobra. I encouraged him to write down what he said. We were talking while he was brainstorming and writing. We got on the subject of Star Wars. Karl told me that "Attack of the Sith" is his favorite movie and then told me some information about Star Wars. I mentioned that it would be a good thing for him to write about sometime. Then I told him that he could write about it now if he wanted to. He did and wrote down three sentences (without punctuation) and a character's name.

He listed two facts he knew about King Cobras after being prompted. When trying to summarize a movie, he listed three facts.

Analysis: Possible Patterns

Karl needed a lot of support when asked to respond to his picture in writing.

He did not seem to summarize what he wanted to communicate about The Revenge of the Sith. Rather his analysis of the information he wanted to share seemed not to be critical information.

Forming letters seems to require a lot of attention; perhaps this is getting in the way of responding in writing in more in-depth ways.

(*continued*)

19

TABLE II.3 Continued

These examples are from Kristin's notes on observations of Karl's text reading. Karl read two leveled books from the Developmental Reading Assessment (DRA) series (Beaver & Carter, 2006): *Game Day* (Beyer, 2006), and *Green Freddie* (Zano, 2006). Kristin's notes refer to the scoring criteria provided by the DRA. She used this scoring criteria to support her analysis of observations.

Responding to Text and Comprehending (Reading)

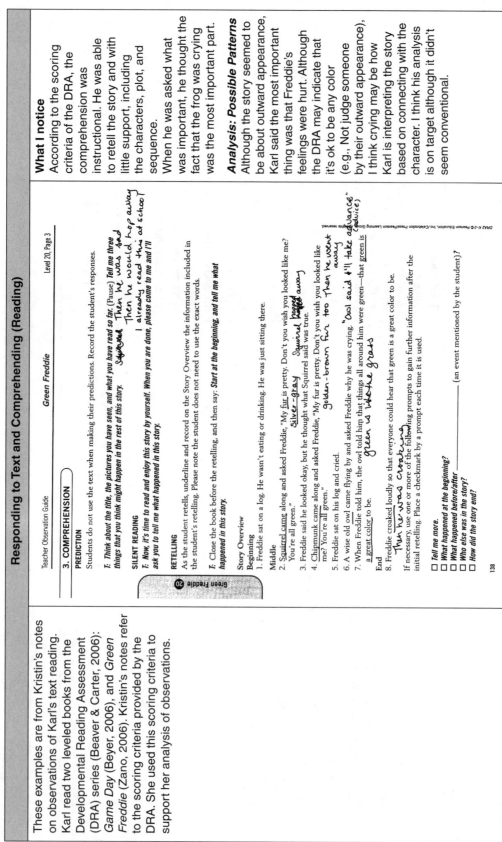

Teacher Observation Guide   *Green Freddie*   Level 20, Page 3

3. COMPREHENSION

PREDICTION

Students do not use the text when making their predictions. Record the student's responses.

T: **Think about the title, the pictures you have seen, and what you have read so far.** (Pause) **Tell me three things that you think might happen in the rest of this story.**

Squirrel   Then he was sad
I already read this at school   Then he would hop away

SILENT READING

T: **Now, it's time to read and enjoy this story by yourself. When you are done, please come to me and I'll ask you to tell me what happened in this story.**

RETELLING

As the student retells, underline and record on the Story Overview the information included in the student's retelling. Please note the student does not need to use the exact words.

T: Close the book before the retelling, and then say: **Start at the beginning, and tell me what happened in this story.**

Story Overview

Beginning

1. Freddie sat on a log. He wasn't eating or drinking. He was just sitting there.

Middle

2. Squirrel came along and asked Freddie, "My fur is pretty. Don't you wish you looked like me? You're all green."   Silver-gray   Squirrel hopped away

3. Freddie said he looked okay, but he thought what Squirrel said was true.

4. Chipmunk came along and asked Freddie, "My fur is pretty. Don't you wish you looked like me? You're all green."   Golden-brown fur too   Then he went away

5. Freddie sat on his log and cried.

6. A wise old owl came flying by and asked Freddie why he was crying. "Owl said I'll take advance" (advice)

7. When Freddie told him, the owl told him that things all around him were green—that green is a great color to be.   green is like the grass

End

8. Freddie croaked loudly so that everyone could hear that green is a great color to be.   Then he was croaking

If necessary, use one or more of the following prompts to gain further information after the initial retelling. Place a checkmark by a prompt each time it is used.

☐ **Tell me more.**
☐ **What happened at the beginning?**
☐ **What happened before/after** _____ (an event mentioned by the student)?
☐ **Who else was in the story?**
☐ **How did the story end?**

138

What I notice

According to the scoring criteria of the DRA, the comprehension was instructional. He was able to retell the story and with little support, including the characters, plot, and sequence.

When he was asked what was important, he thought the fact that the frog was crying was the most important part.

Analysis: Possible Patterns

Although the story seemed to be about outward appearance, Karl said the most important thing was that Freddie's feelings were hurt. Although the DRA may indicate that it's ok to be any color (e.g., Not judge someone by their outward appearance), I think crying may be how Karl is interpreting the story based on connecting with the character. I think his analysis is on target although it didn't seem conventional.

(continued)

TABLE II.3 Continued

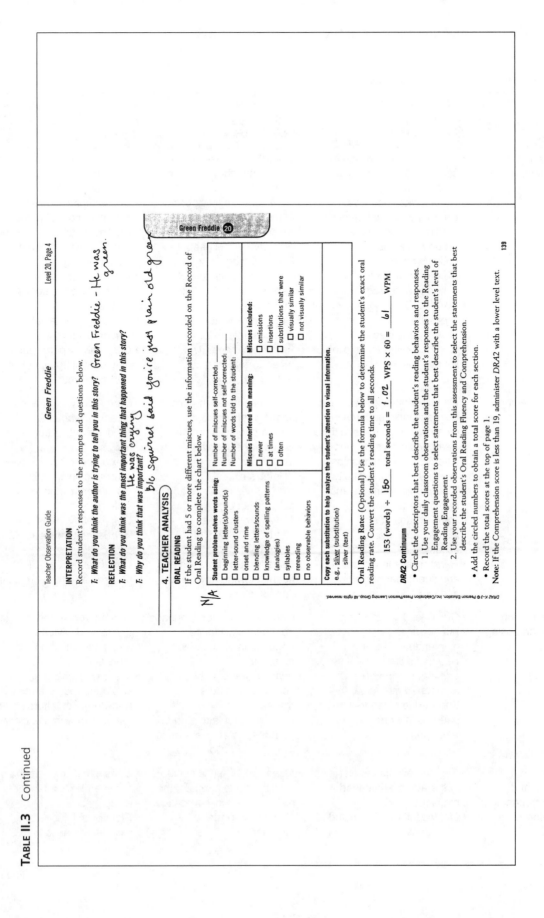

Teacher Observation Guide   *Green Freddie*   Level 20, Page 4

INTERPRETATION

Record student's responses to the prompts and questions below.

T: *What do you think the author is trying to tell you in this story?* Green Freddie - He was green.

REFLECTION

T: *What do you think was the most important thing that happened in this story?*
He was crying

T: *Why do you think that was important?*
b/c Squirrel said you're just plain old green

4. TEACHER ANALYSIS

ORAL READING

If the student had 5 or more different miscues, use the information recorded on the Record of Oral Reading to complete the chart below.

N/A

Student problem-solves words using:	Number of miscues self-corrected: _____
☐ beginning letter(s)/sound(s)	Number of miscues not self-corrected: _____
☐ letter-sound clusters	Number of words told to the student: _____
☐ onset and rime	
☐ blending letters/sounds	**Miscues interfered with meaning:** **Miscues included:**
☐ knowledge of spelling patterns	☐ never ☐ omissions
(analogies)	☐ at times ☐ insertions
☐ syllables	☐ often ☐ substitutions that were
☐ rereading	☐ visually similar
☐ no observable behaviors	☐ not visually similar

Copy each substitution to help analyze the student's attention to visual information.
e.g., silver (substitution)
    silver (text)

Oral Reading Rate: (Optional) Use the formula below to determine the student's exact oral reading rate. Convert the student's reading time to all seconds.

153 (words) ÷ 150 total seconds = 1.02 WPS × 60 = 61 WPM

DRA2 Continuum

- Circle the descriptors that best describe the student's reading behaviors and responses.
  1. Use your daily classroom observations and the student's responses to the Reading Engagement questions to select statements that best describe the student's level of Reading Engagement.
  2. Use your recorded observations from this assessment to select the statements that best describe the student's Oral Reading Fluency and Comprehension.
- Add the circled numbers to obtain a total score for each section.
- Record the total scores at the top of page 1.

Note: If the Comprehension score is less than 19, administer *DRA2* with a lower level text.

139

Green Freddie 20

TABLE II.4 Kristen's Rubric for Karl's Assessments

	Developing and Instructionally Dependent	On the Way to Independence	Independent and Needs More Challenge
Conversations and Inventories	• *Seldom* makes positive comments about the use of literacy in life. • Often makes negative comments about perceived reading/writing competence. • *Seldom* talks about books/writing. • *Rarely* initiates self-selection of books and reads. • *Rarely* writes about personal interests. • *Rarely* perceives reading/writing as enjoyable literacy events.	• *Sometimes* makes positive comments about the use of literacy in life. • *Sometimes* makes positive comments about perceived reading/writing competence. • *Sometimes* talks about books/writing. • *Sometimes* initiates self-selection of books and reads. • *Sometimes* writes about personal interests. • Perceives reading/writing as enjoyable literacy events.	• *Frequently* makes positive comments about the use of literacy in life. • *Consistently* makes positive comments about perceived reading/writing competence. • *Frequently* talks about books/writing. • *Frequently* initiates self-selection of books and reads. • *Frequently* writes about personal interests. • *Consistently* perceives reading/writing as enjoyable literacy events
Oral Reading	• *Often* invents text, searches for predictable patterns in meaning, language structure. • *Searches* exclusively for letter/sound relationships at every point of difficulty. • *Infrequently* monitors and self-corrects. • *Rarely* reads at an instructional level of accuracy. • *Rarely* reads in a phrased and fluent manner; slow and word by word.	• *Often* integrates meaning, language structure, and grapho-phonic information. • *Sometimes* searches for different sources of information. • *Sometimes* monitors and self-corrects. • *Usually* reads at an instructional level of accuracy. • *Usually* reads phrased and fluent, slowing down and speeding up.	• *Consistently* integrates meaning, language structure, and grapho-phonic information. • *Flexibly* searches for different sources of information. • *Consistently* monitors and self-corrects. • *Consistently* reads at an instructional and easy level of accuracy. • *Consistently* reads in a phrased and fluent manner.
Constructing and Composing	• Oral and/or written language *rarely* evidence negotiation of intended message. • *Seems hesitant* to initiate problem solving of ways to record a message. • Knowledge of letters and/or patterns in words *is emerging*.	• Oral and/or written language *sometimes* evidence negotiation of intended message. • *Initiates some* problem solving to record a message. • Knowledge of letters and/or patterns in words *seems to be in construction*.	• Oral and/or written language *consistently* evidence negotiation of intended message. • *Initiates flexible* problem solving to record a message. • Knowledge of letters and/or patterns in words *is clear*.
Responding to Text and Comprehending: Summarizing	• *Seldom* reflects the gist of the author's intended message. • *Limited* information included in response.	• *Often* makes sense to the child but seldom reflects the gist of the author's message. • *Relevant* important information included in response.	• *Consistently* reflects the gist of the author's intended message. • *Significant* information included in response.

(continued)

Table II.4   Continued

	Developing and Instructionally Dependent	On the Way to Independence	Independent and Needs More Challenge
Responding to Text and Comprehending: Analyzing	• *Seldom* determines critical features of story structures in fiction (e.g., characters, setting, plot) and expository text structures in nonfiction (description, sequence, cause/effect). • *Unimportant* features of text emphasized.	• *Sometimes* determines critical features of story structures in fiction (e.g., characters, setting, plot) and expository text structures in nonfiction (description, sequence, cause/effect). • *Some* relevant features of text emphasized.	• *Consistently* determines critical features of story structures in fiction (e.g., characters, setting, plot) and expository text structures in nonfiction (description, sequence, cause/effect). • *Critical* features of the text emphasized.
Responding to Text and Comprehending: Synthesizing	• *Rarely* combines/connects multiple sources of information in a coherent fashion. • *Rarely* draws conclusions based on pertinent information. • Pulls together *irrelevant* information.	• *Sometimes* combines/ connects multiple sources of information in coherent fashion. • *Sometimes* draws conclusions based on pertinent information in a coherent fashion • Pulls together *some relevant* information.	• *Consistently* combines/ connects multiple sources of information in a coherent fashion. • *Sometimes* draws conclusions based on pertinent information in a coherent fashion. • Pulls together *very relevant* information.
Responding to Text and Comprehending: Evaluating	• *Rarely* takes a critical stance toward the text. • *Seldom and/or inappropriately* judges the quality of information available in order to make inferences.	• *Often* takes a critical stance toward the text. • *Often* and/or appropriately judges the quality of information available in order to make inferences.	• *Consistently* takes a critical stance toward the text. • *Consistently* and/or appropriately judges the quality of information available in order to make inferences.

section is shaded to identify where Kristin determined Karl's present processing to be. In some areas, she highlighted two columns, indicating she was tentative about making a categorization and probably needed to do more assessment.

STEP 5:   *Summarize.* Write a brief summary of how you see the child responding and comprehending. In this summary, try to provide sound rationales for the conclusions drawn from the assessments. Kristin gathered her data as part of a course assignment. She used adaptations of interviews based on the developmental reading assessment (Beaver & Carter, 2006). Here is Kristin's summary:

Karl seems to be developing an identity as a reader. His oral read processing seems like he's on the way to independence with perhaps more challenge needed in terms of text difficulty. When composing or responding to text by writing, he seems to be developing and instructionally dependent. On the DRA when asked to retell and answer questions, his comprehending seemed to be on the way to independence and/or a need for more challenge. It seems his reading is stronger than his writing, but in both dimensions, he sees literacy as copying words or saying words as opposed to thoughtful literacy.

PLANNING INSTRUCTION

Think about one or two goals that would help the child's literacy processing become more complex. Here are Kristin's goals for Karl:

- Karl will learn how reading and writing affect his learning and life in order to develop a positive literary identity.
- Karl will use writing to respond deeply to his life and text.

Table II.5 connects each lesson with the assessment areas. This table indicates which of the 20 lessons connect, particularly for students who are instructionally dependent in that area. Karl is particularly instructionally dependent related to literate identity and responding in writing. So four lessons focus on both of those areas: Diary Writing, Readers' Theater, Sketch-to-Stretch, and Literacy Talk Show. Because all of the lessons relate to comprehension, Karl would benefit from all of them adapted to his needs.

EFFECTIVE TEACHING

Effective teachers provide clear demonstrations and scaffold new learning (Cazden, 2001; Moll, 1990), gradually releasing control (see Figure II.2). Students transform thinking (Bruner & Weinreich-Haste, 1987) through calibrated assistance where language becomes a tool (Bruner, 1990; Vygotsky, Rieber, & Carton, 1987). The language of demonstrations becomes the speech (Tharp & Gallimore, 1988; Wertsch, 1985) guiding new learning. The teacher encourages the student's engagement and releases control verbally (less talk), physically (lets go of the book or pencil), and proximally (moves away from the child's side) (Clay, 1979, 1982; Dorn & Soffos, 2001; Dyson, 1981; Wood, 1998).

Given the opportunity, students construct processing systems as they try out something new, monitor performance, and self-correct as needed. With opportunities to practice the new learning during literacy events, talking, writing, or reading, the processing systems become fluent and flexible, freeing up the learner's attention to focus on new demonstrations. Good teaching is knowing when to increase the challenge, help the child solve problems, and/or provide a clear demonstration at a certain point to relieve frustration (Gambrell et al., 2007; Tharp & Gallimore, 1988).

As shown in Figure II.2, teaching changes by releasing control as the child demonstrates an increasingly sophisticated processing system. Thus if the analysis of the assessment tools in specific areas fits the criteria under the "Developing and Instructionally Dependent" heading in the rubric, clear demonstrations during the literacy lessons will be particularly important. Furthermore, students need engaging, positive experiences with instructional-level text or writing. If books are too hard, frustration results, and we unknowingly exacerbate the student's passive stance (Clay, 1991). Authentic learning experiences are critical for students' developing sense of identity, thus helping them select topics and instructional books accessible and relevant to their lives.

If the assessment indicates criteria in the middle column, "On the Way to Independence," think carefully about ways of using language to provide help or "prompting" during the lessons. As teachers, our nature is to offer support to ensure success. However, sometimes we unknowingly control too much, not noticing the

TABLE II.5 Lesson Selection Guide: Linking Assessment Data to Model Lessons

	Conversations and Inventories	Oral Reading	Constructing and Composing	Responding to Text and Comprehending: Summarizing	Responding to Text and Comprehending: Analyzing	Responding to Text and Comprehending: Synthesis	Responding to Text and Comprehending: Evaluating
Anticipation Guide	*	*					*
Cause-and-Effect Map		*			*	*	
Character Map		*			*	*	*
Character Shield		*			*	*	*
Diary Writing	*		*	*			
KWL	*	*					*
Learning Logs	*	*	*	*		*	
Literary News Report	*	*		*	*		*
Literary Report Card	*				*		*
Literary Sociogram		*			*	*	*
Literary Talk Show	*	*	*	*	*	*	*
Main Idea Map		*			*	*	
Open and Closed Sort	*	*			*	*	
Readers' Theater	*	*	*	*		*	
Shared Writing			*				
Sketch-to-Stretch	*		*	*	*	*	*
Story Map		*			*		
Summary Pyramid			*	*	*		
Venn Diagram		*			*		
Vocabulary Web		*			*		

FIGURE II.2 Relationship Between Teaching and Assessment Rubric

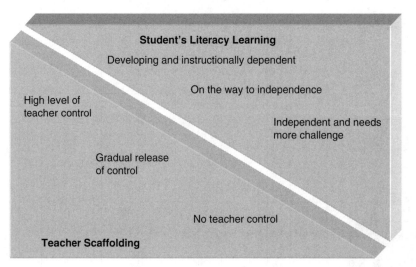

ways students initiate and make approximations. A student's partially correct responses provide powerful teaching opportunities to help rather than tell the child the right answer.

Finally, if the assessment indicates criteria in the "Independent and Needs More Challenge" column, think about ways of increasing the complexity of the lesson. This strategy may include exploring a different genre in reading and writing, increasing the difficulty level of the text, and/or shifting the context in which the learning occurs to teach for flexibility.

EFFECTIVE TEACHING OF BILINGUAL AND ENGLISH LANGUAGE LEARNERS

The literacy lessons note adaptations for bilingual and English language learners. A vast research base supports effective practice with this population. The following is a brief representation of key research-based elements to bear in mind when planning teaching for diverse language learners' literacy lessons. First, ensure students have ample time to negotiate meaning and construct understandings in conversation. A student's first language is not a deficit. It's through conversations with peers and teachers that students' language grows. Encourage opportunities for students to use their first languages to construct oral/written responses. Accept and encourage approximations because students learn through meaningful interaction, not correction. Thus planning and ensuring meaningful conversation between students and with teachers is a critical aspect of effective teaching.

Second, provide examples of texts portraying characters and/or settings that the student can relate to linguistically and culturally. This is appropriate for all children but especially important for this population. Text representing unique cultural backgrounds provides a powerful foundation for thoughtful literacy.

Finally, encourage various means of symbol making using pictures and different mediums to express meanings from text or to plan written text. Students can see, feel, hear, and act out language construct systems that are generative and expand them. If we limit responses to paper-and-pencil written responses, we unknowingly limit English language learners' opportunities to learn and thus become thoughtfully literate. In each Literacy Lesson are specific suggestions related to the lesson and this population; however, based on these recommendations, we are sure effective teachers will construct many more.

In the next section, we introduce twenty model lessons designed to support the student's comprehension of text. Table II.5 provides a selection guide for linking assessment data with model lessons for teaching.

Part III
Literacy Lessons

Twenty model lessons are included in this section. Each lesson is designed to make the process that expert teachers engage in as they plan effective instruction visible to novice teachers. Lessons are organized according to how expert teachers think about connecting assessment to instruction, concisely detailing the when, what, why, how, and who of teaching reading comprehension. Examples of students' work across grade levels are provided.

In the margin of each lesson, a quick reference to the dimensions of assessment and related tools is provided (as detailed previously in Table II.1).

Begin by revisiting the processes for linking assessment to comprehension instruction. Figure III.1 provides an overview of the six steps discussed in Part II.

FIGURE III.1   Overview of Linking Assessment

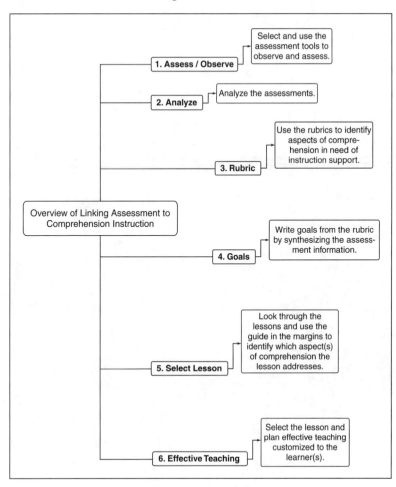

Lesson Plan 1

ANTICIPATION GUIDE

WHAT *is an anticipation guide?*

A series of statements that students choose to agree or disagree with prior to reading a text

WHY *engage students in this lesson?*

The lesson will help students:

- Initiate a critical stance toward reading.
- Make decisions using relevant information.
- Search for information while reading.
- Support evaluation of text with evidence.

WHEN *might you use this lesson?*

Assessment analysis reveals that the student(s):

- Rarely anticipate or predict prior to reading.
- Adopt a passive, rather than a critical stance, to text reading.
- Rarely respond to the content of the text after reading.

HOW *do you set up and teach this lesson?*

Instructional steps:

1. Demonstrate the process of making predictions about a text prior to reading.
2. Before the lesson, identify a major point or main ideas to emphasize in the text. Write 5 to 10 opinion statements on chart paper or handout. Include a balance of true-and-false statements and blank space next to each statement for students' responses.
3. Working individually or in small groups, ask students to indicate agreement "+" or disagreement "−" with each statement.
4. Discuss statements and students' responses.

ASSESSMENT DIMENSIONS

Conversations/Inventories
Tools
  ⇨ Conversations
  ⇨ Surveys/Checklists
  ⇨ Observations
Link to Comprehending
  o Attitudes
  o Interests

Oral Reading
Tools
  ⇨ Running records
  ⇨ Miscue analysis
  ⇨ Informal reading inventory
Link to Comprehending
  o Decision making
  o Fluency

Constructing and Composing
Tools
  ⇨ Writing samples
  ⇨ Conversations
Link to Comprehending
  o Negotiating messages through text
  o Problem solving
  o Knowledge of letters and/or word patterns

Responding to Text
Tools
  ⇨ Conversations
  ⇨ Retelling
  ⇨ Oral and written and responses to open ended activities
Link to Comprehending
  o Analysis
  o Synthesis
  o Summarizing
  o Evaluating

31

5. Read aloud the text or ask students to read the text aloud.
6. Ask students to look for the statements that support, contradict, or modify their opinions during their reading of text. Students then return to the guide to record their second responses with "+" or "−."
7. Discuss reasons for initial opinions and reasons for changes in opinion.
8. Shift level of support provided based on students' background knowledge and abilities.

WHO *will benefit from this instruction, and how will you expect students to learn?*

Individual Instruction:

- Model through a "think-aloud" the process and reasoning for your agreement or disagreement with statements.

Small Group Instruction:

- Prepare a guide to support students during guided reading lessons or literature circle discussions.

Whole Class Instruction:

- Model the process to the whole class. Read the text aloud and lead small groups in discussion and prediction process.

Bilingual Student(s) Instruction:

- Extend students' understanding of the second-language concepts presented in the text through hands-on opportunities, videos, and the use of pictures to generate discussion.

Materials

Text related to student interest and curriculum goals, anticipation guide statements on a handout or large chart, and markers.

ANTICIPATION GUIDE
A THIRD GRADER'S WRITTEN RESPONSE

Anticipation Guide

For a Good Cause by Patricia Baehr

Agreement Before Reading	Agreement After the Reading	Question
		Use + or - for agreement or disagreement
—	—	Habitat for Humanity is a cause that raises a great deal of negative concern in the community.
+	+	US President Jimmy Carter is a supporter of the Habitat for Humanity cause.
+	+	Millard and Linda Fuller, the creators of Habitat for Humanity, were kind and caring people.
—	—	Volunteers in the community do not care about Habitat for Humanity.
+	—	Habitat for Humanity has decreased over the past 30 years.

1. it is helping people to have shelter.
2. he bad intres and na is suporter.
3. yes, because if they creaated it so probly they are kind and caring people.
4. no, cause why would they do it if they don't care.
5. no, because they worked more over the past 30years and have done more.

LESSON PLAN  2

CAUSE-AND-EFFECT MAP

WHAT *is a cause-and-effect map?*

A graphic organizer that supports students' analysis of the cause and effect of a problem found in fiction and nonfiction texts

WHY *engage students in this lesson?*

The lesson will help students:

- Monitor and search for information while reading.
- Determine the critical relationships between events in a text in order to draw conclusions.

WHEN *might you use this lesson?*

Assessment analysis reveals that the student(s):

- Write stories with a simple beginning/middle/end.
- Talk about events in the text without connections.
- Experience difficulty expressing reason(s) for events in text.

Response to text example:

> Student 1: "I wonder why the colonists threw out all the tea at the Boston Tea Party?"
> Student 2: "Maybe they were mad."

HOW *do you set up and teach this lesson?*

Instructional steps:

1. Select a text to be read aloud, preferably one that has several clear examples of cause and effect.
2. Read the text aloud to the students.
3. Pause at places in the text that offer good demonstrations of cause and effect. Engage the students in a conversation about the text. Instruct them to identify the cause and effects shown in the text.

ASSESSMENT DIMENSIONS

Conversations/Inventories
Tools
- ⇨ Conversations
- ⇨ Surveys/Checklists
- ⇨ Observations

Link to Comprehending
- ○ Attitudes
- ○ Interests

Oral Reading
Tools
- ⇨ Running records
- ⇨ Miscue analysis
- ⇨ Informal reading inventory

Link to Comprehending
- ○ Decision making
- ○ Fluency

Constructing and Composing
Tools
- ⇨ Writing samples
- ⇨ Conversations

Link to Comprehending
- ○ Negotiating messages through text
- ○ Problem solving
- ○ Knowledge of letters and/or word patterns

Responding to Text
Tools
- ⇨ Conversations
- ⇨ Retelling
- ⇨ Oral and written and responses to open ended activities

Link to Comprehending
- ○ Analysis
- ○ Synthesis
- ○ Summarizing
- ○ Evaluating

4. Record the cause and effect on the map.
5. After each cause and effect is recorded, discuss in detail why this was the cause to an identified problem.
6. Continue the process until the cause and effect is recorded for each section.
7. Conclude by having the students review the problems of the entire book and the causes.
8. Have students select a text to read. Engage them in discussion about elements of the text that are key when selecting the texts.
9. As students read their text, instruct them to use a map to record the problems and the reasons for the problems.
10. Ask each individual to share his or her completed cause-and-effect map as appropriate.

WHO *will benefit from this instruction, and how will you expect students to learn?*

Individual Instruction:

- Work one on one with a student after reading the text aloud or independent reading.

Small Group Instruction:

- Use maps during guided reading or literature study group instruction.

Whole Class Instruction:

- Have the whole class work collaboratively in small groups developing a map based on a book read aloud.

Bilingual Student(s) Instruction:

- Use examples and texts from student's native land to demonstrate cause and effect. Example: For older students, create a cause-and-effect map for the politics of their home country.

Materials

Texts that include a cause and effect and an example of a completed map for demonstration.

CAUSE AND EFFECT MAP
A SECOND GRADER'S WRITTEN RESPONSE

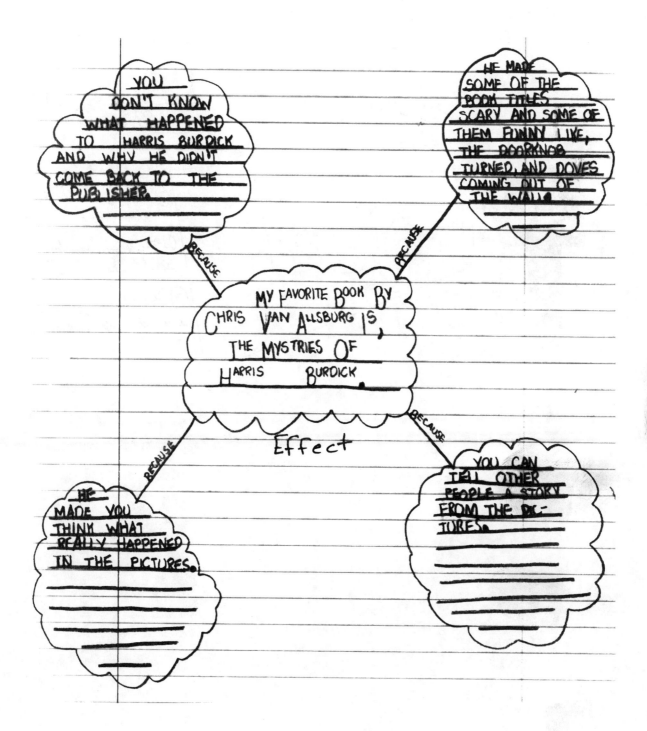

YOU DON'T KNOW WHAT HAPPENED TO HARRIS BURDICK AND WHY HE DIDN'T COME BACK TO THE PUBLISHER.

HE MADE SOME OF THE BOOK TITLES SCARY AND SOME OF THEM FUNNY LIKE, THE DOORKNOB TURNED, AND DOVES COMING OUT OF THE WALLS.

BECAUSE

BECAUSE

MY FAVORITE BOOK BY CHRIS VAN ALLSBURG IS, THE MYSTRIES OF HARRIS BURDICK.

Effect

BECAUSE

BECAUSE

HE MADE YOU THINK WHAT REALLY HAPPENED IN THE PICTURES.

YOU CAN TELL OTHER PEOPLE A STORY FROM THE PICTURES.

John Hancock

Friendly

① He give children money
② He gave party at his house
③ He made jokes with the other men.

LESSON PLAN 3

CHARACTER MAP

WHAT *is a character map?*

A graphic organizer used to record a character's traits and supporting actions

WHY *engage students in this lesson?*

The lesson will help students:

- Monitor and search for information about characters while reading.
- Determine critical features of a character's personality.
- Synthesize and evaluate a character's actions in order to infer implicit traits.

WHEN *might you use this lesson?*

Assessment analysis reveals that the student(s):

- Converse about characters and focus on recall or specific details to "answer" questions.
- Describe a character/historical figure inaccurately, such as "mean," when the character's actions do not reflect this trait.
- Resist taking an evaluative stance toward characters.

HOW *do you set up and teach this lesson?*

Instructional steps:

1. Select a text to read aloud with interesting character(s).
2. Present and discuss parts of the character map (traits with supporting behaviors).
3. Discuss and define traits (e.g., loyal, curious, proud, daring).
4. Brainstorm a list of possible character traits (words describing the "inside" of a character or his or her personality).
5. Discuss how specific actions or behaviors reveal traits of a character. For example, from the story "Little Red Riding Hood," the wolf dressed in Grandma's clothes is an action and reflects the trait of being clever. The

ASSESSMENT DIMENSIONS

Conversations/Inventories
Tools
- ⇨ Conversations
- ⇨ Surveys/Checklists
- ⇨ Observations

Link to Comprehending
- ○ Attitudes
- ○ Interests

Oral Reading
Tools
- ⇨ Running records
- ⇨ Miscue analysis
- ⇨ Informal reading inventory

Link to Comprehending
- ○ Decision making
- ○ Fluency

Constructing and Composing
Tools
- ⇨ Writing samples
- ⇨ Conversations

Link to Comprehending
- ○ Negotiating messages through text
- ○ Problem solving
- ○ Knowledge of letters and/or word patterns

Responding to Text
Tools
- ⇨ Conversations
- ⇨ Retelling
- ⇨ Oral and written and responses to open ended activities

Link to Comprehending
- ○ Analysis
- ○ Synthesis
- ○ Summarizing
- ○ Evaluating

39

more actions or behaviors that support a trait, the more the trait applies to that character.

6. Read the text aloud.
7. Demonstrate how to complete a character map using one character from the text on chart paper, overhead projector, or white/blackboard.
8. Provide student(s) with a character map form. Student(s) will individually or in groups complete a character map on a second character in the text. Provide extra copies of the text for small group work.

WHO *will benefit from this instruction, and how will you expect students to learn?*

Individual Instruction:

- Support the student in constructing a map of his or her traits before engaging in an analysis of a text character.

Small Group Instruction:

- Provide specific support through the book introduction related to character development to help students attend to new aspects in texts related to characters.

Whole Class Instruction:

- Ask students to work collaboratively in small groups exploring different characters in stories. Groups discuss similarities and differences and analyze results.

Bilingual Student(s) Instruction:

- Use drawing and/or role playing to support analysis of characters. Pair students with a native-language speaker to support development of the map.

Materials

Text for introduction and character map construction (multiple copies for small group/whole class instruction), pens or markers, and copies of character map form.

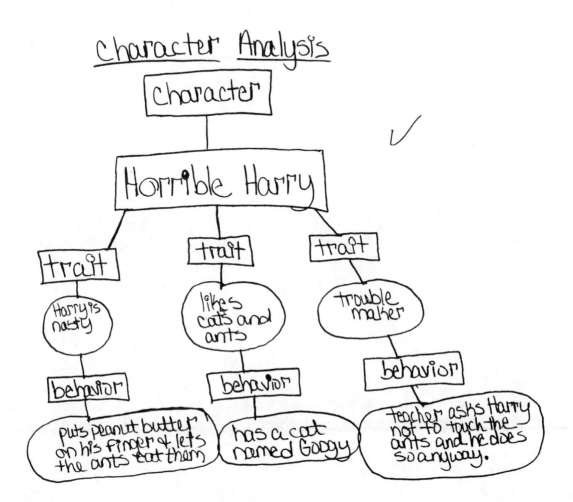

Character Analysis

Character

Horrible Harry

trait — Harry is nasty — behavior — puts peanut butter on his finger & lets the ants eat them

trait — likes cats and ants — behavior — has a cat named Googy

trait — trouble maker — behavior — teacher asks Harry not to touch the ants and he does so anyway.

Alexander and the Terrible, Horrible, No Good, Very Bad Day

Lesson Plan 4

Character Shield

WHAT *is a character shield?*

A visual display of critical features of a character (see Figure III.2, page 44)

WHY *engage students in this lesson?*

The lesson will help students:

- Determine critical features of a character.
- Record evidence of character features in visual form.
- Search and monitor for meaning while reading.

WHEN *might you use this lesson?*

Assessment analysis reveals that the student(s):

- Describe characters in superficial ways.
- Comment or make inferences regarding the characters.

Response to text example:

> Teacher: What do you think about the wolf?
> Student: He's bad.

HOW *do you set up and teach this lesson?*

Instructional steps:

1. Select a text with multiple characters.
2. Introduce the character shield as a way to help the students focus on more in-depth information about characters.
3. Show a blank shield. Define each section (character's name, family, friend, wish/goal, feelings, and resolution).
4. Read the text aloud.
5. Demonstrate how to fill in the character shield.

FIGURE III.2   Character Shield

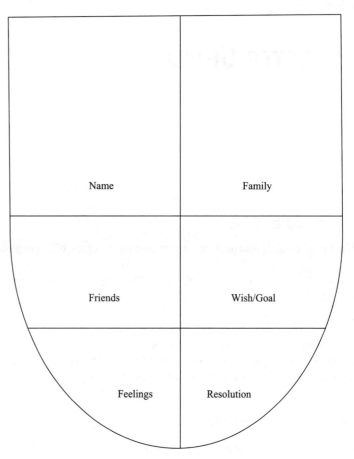

6. Support students in developing a character shield on another character in the story.
7. Share and compare shields.

WHO *will benefit from this instruction, and how will you expect students to learn?*

Individual Instruction:

- Students may select a familiar text character and complete a character shield.

Small Group Instruction:

- Groups may complete a character shield together. Each group in the class works on a different character, and the characters of the entire story are displayed together.

Whole Class Instruction:

- Complete a character shield as a whole class as a way to generate discussion beyond the facts.

Bilingual Student(s) Instruction:

- Provide extra conversational, descriptive support.
- Allow students to draw and talk about each part of the shield.

Materials

A fiction or nonfiction text with strong development of multiple characters.

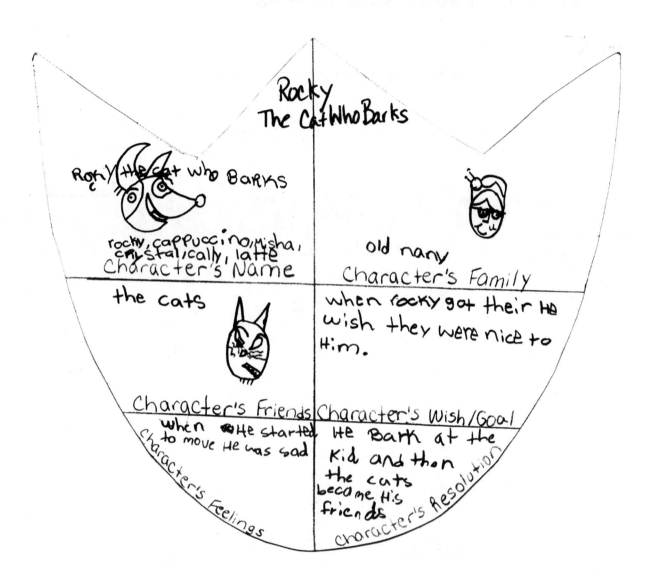

Rocky
The Cat Who Barks

Rocky the cat who Barks

rocky, cappuccino, misha,
crystalically, latte
Character's Name

old nany
Character's Family

the cats
Character's Friends

when rocky got their He
wish they were nice to
Him.
Character's Wish/Goal

when He started
to move He was sad
Character's Feelings

He Bark at the
Kid and then
the cats
became His
friends
Character's Resolution

DIARY WRITING

WHAT *is diary writing?*

A written text recording personal responses to reading

WHY *engage students in this lesson?*

The lesson will help students:

- Perceive reading and writing in school as personally relevant.
- Negotiate intended messages and record in self-selected forms.
- Search for ways to record responses to text.

WHEN *might you use this lesson*

Assessment analysis reveals that the student(s):

- May not view literacy as important in their lives.
- Resist constructing and composing written messages.

HOW *do you set up and use this lesson?*

Instructional steps:

1. Select one expository or nonfiction text.
2. Read the text to the student(s). For younger students (grades K–2), read the text aloud. For older students (grades 3–8), read the text aloud or provide multiple copies for independent reading.
3. Engage students in a discussion about common characteristics of the text. Extend the discussion to feelings, reactions, thoughts, experiences, and so on, evoked by the text read.
4. Model diary writing for the students. Use simple language and a casual style. Write in first person: "I" or "me." Record the students' reactions to the text.
5. Ask students to select a text to read that interests them. Engage them in discussion about elements of the text that are key when selecting the texts. For example, tell the students to select books that interest them. This will promote feelings, reactions, thoughts, and experiences about the text.

47

6. Students will work collaboratively to identify, discuss, and write about their feelings, reactions, thoughts, and/or experiences that connect to the text.
7. Students will share their completed diary writing as appropriate.

WHO *will benefit from this instruction, and how will you expect students to learn?*

Individual Instruction:

- Demonstrate and write next to the students, or take dictation from the student, demonstrating how to make a personal connection to the text.
- Allow the student to use a different medium, like paint or clay.

Small Group Instruction:

- Students may discuss how they relate to the text through their feelings, reactions, experiences, and thoughts.

Whole Class Instruction:

- Students may work collaboratively in small groups to construct diary writings. In this instance, the class would use the word "we" in place of "I" or "me." Small groups may present to the entire class.

Bilingual Student(s) Instruction:

- Provide students with samples of diary writings in their first language.

Materials

Two texts about interesting topics (one for demonstration, multiple copies for independent work), a chart large enough for group demonstration, and plain paper.

Dog's

I read a book about a Dog that is about a big dog hes a Great Dane! a Great Dane is a very big dog and is a very strong dog to! Great danes are probley like 5feet on there 4 legs but on there hine legs they are 10feet!

PeNDRagON: The lost City of Faar

When I was Reading the section about
when the habitat's crash, and the
other habitat is MysterIously Poisioed and
sPaders Father is Killed, I felt sad
that sPader has to have Face all of the ~~responsibili~~
responsibilities of a traveler,

LESSON PLAN 6

KWL

WHAT *is KWL?*

A graphic organizer used to record *what we think we know* (K), *what we want to know* (W), and *what we learned* (L)

WHY *engage students in this lesson?*

The lesson will help students:

- Take an active stance toward the text.
- Converse and connect personally to the text prior to reading.
- Judge the quality of information while reading.

WHEN *might you use this lesson?*

Assessment analysis reveals that the student(s):

- Respond in what appears to be a passive way to text.
- Neglect meaning when reading expository text.
- Offer comments to other students regarding specific concepts in texts.

Oral reading example:

"The Three Little Pigs"

Text: "The little pig said, 'Not by the hair of my chinney chin chin.'"
Student reads, "(–)(–) hippo (–) 'No but the her of my chip chip chip.'"

HOW *do you set up and use this lesson?*

Instructional steps:

1. Select at least two texts (trade books, article from magazines, newspapers, websites).
2. Present the topic and help students focus on their current knowledge of the topic.

ASSESSMENT DIMENSIONS

Conversations/Inventories
Tools
- ⇨ Conversations
- ⇨ Surveys/Checklists
- ⇨ Observations
Link to Comprehending
- ○ Attitudes
- ○ Interests

Oral Reading
Tools
- ⇨ Running records
- ⇨ Miscue analysis
- ⇨ Informal reading inventory
Link to Comprehending
- ○ Decision making
- ○ Fluency

Constructing and Composing
Tools
- ⇨ Writing samples
- ⇨ Conversations
Link to Comprehending
- ○ Negotiating messages through text
- ○ Problem solving
- ○ Knowledge of letters and/or word patterns

Responding to Text
Tools
- ⇨ Conversations
- ⇨ Retelling
- ⇨ Oral and written and responses to open ended activities
Link to Comprehending
- ○ Analysis
- ○ Synthesis
- ○ Summarizing
- ○ Evaluating

51

3. Lead students as they activate prior knowledge and record all responses under the "What We Think We Know" section of the chart.
4. As students generate responses, encourage them to extend their thinking and provide evidence.
5. Guide the students as they generate questions or topics they want to find out about under the "What We Want to Know" section.
6. Through interest inventories and curriculum documents, select a topic.
7. Read the text aloud. Encourage students to comment on their ideas.
8. Clarify and refine their developing understanding of key concepts.
9. After reading, guide the discussion to choose new concepts from the text, confirm concepts they already knew, and clarify or refine any ideas that may have been inaccurate.
10. Modify the next column if appropriate for instructional purposes with "What We Still Want to Know."
11. Students may use the strategy independently as they read new texts.

WHO will benefit from this instruction, and how will you expect students to learn?

Individual Instruction:

- Students may self-select topic of interest and use a KWL to set goals for their own learning.

Small Group Instruction:

- Small groups work collaboratively on development of a KWL chart.

Whole Class Instruction:

- Select a textbook chapter or nonfiction trade book and model the process of using a KWL chart before students begin working in small groups or individually.

Bilingual Student(s) Instruction:

- Compete a KWL on a topic of high interest.

Materials

Nonfiction text (multiple copies for small group/whole class instruction), pens or markers, and copies of KWL form.

KWL
A FOURTH GRADER'S WRITTEN RESPONSE

Water cycle

KWL

What I Know	What I Want to Know	What I Learned
it never stops	Where does it start up or down?	underground water
it is a cycle	what happends to all of the waste	same water as dinosuars
	what does the water have in it	evaPoration consiation
		Pesipitation co'
		Collection
		Self clersing

LEARNING LOGS

WHAT *are learning logs?*

A written record of relevant information in and reactions to text recorded while reading

WHY *engage students in this lesson?*

The lesson will help students:

- Record personal responses.
- Determine critical features of the text.
- Negotiate an intended message to be recorded.

WHEN *might you use this lesson?*

Assessment analysis reveals that the student(s):

- Focus on literal details when reading texts.
- Provide a meager amount of new concepts in expository writing.
- Do not connect new information learned across text readings.
- See expository text as difficult and are reluctant to read textbooks.

Response to text example:

Teacher: What do you think about Thomas Jefferson?
Student: I don't know.
Teacher: What do you know about Thomas Jefferson?
Student: I think he was president?

HOW *do you set up and use this lesson?*

Instructional steps:

1. Select a text to be read aloud, preferably one that can be broken into logical blocks. Short nonfiction articles work well to use as an introduction.
2. Read the text to the students and conduct a think-aloud as you complete a learning log in front of the students in the following manner.

ASSESSMENT DIMENSIONS

Conversations/Inventories
Tools
⇨ Conversations
⇨ Surveys/Checklists
⇨ Observations
Link to Comprehending
○ Attitudes
○ Interests

Oral Reading
Tools
⇨ Running records
⇨ Miscue analysis
⇨ Informal reading inventory
Link to Comprehending
○ Decision making
○ Fluency

Constructing and Composing
Tools
⇨ Writing samples
⇨ Conversations
Link to Comprehending
○ Negotiating messages through text
○ Problem solving
○ Knowledge of letters and/or word patterns

Responding to Text
Tools
⇨ Conversations
⇨ Retelling
⇨ Oral and written and responses to open ended activities
Link to Comprehending
○ Analysis
○ Synthesis
○ Summarizing
○ Evaluating

55

3. Stop at the end of the first section.
4. Ask, "What is important about what I just read?" Record a list of ideas/concepts.
5. Next, ask, "What do I think or feel about what I just read?" Record personal responses. Then draw a line to indicate section breaks.
6. A vertical T chart may also be used with the two questions at the top of each column.
7. Demonstrate two or three sections.
8. Have student complete a section in small groups and share and compare. Students then read another text independently and complete a learning log. The end goal is a strategic way of responding in an ongoing way to text.

WHO will benefit from this instruction, and how will you expect students to learn?

Individual Instruction:

- Individuals may use learning logs for self-selected research projects based on interest to increase motivation.

Small Group Instruction:

- Use as a resource for guided reading instruction of nonfiction text.

Whole Class Instruction:

- After initial demonstrations, create routines in which learning logs are shared periodically as a whole class.

Bilingual Student(s) Instruction:

- Encourage extended conversation and use of illustrations in learning logs.

Materials

Expository texts, chart paper for demonstration, and composition books or spirals for long-term use.

- Stephen King - #1 bestselling auth
- three popular books and many more
- writes horror books
- most made into movies
- when born and where born
- relatives
- anything that influenced or scarred h
- where went to school
- anything significant that would affect his writing career

Insomnia was a pretty good book overall. It has a lot of twists and turns. Stephen King really keeps the reader interested. I would recommend it to anyone who can handle strong language, some blood and gore, and violence. I would rank this book a 9 out of 10.

You have an entire rainbow of vocabulary. Do you use it commonly?

Where did you get the idea or influence for Insomnia?

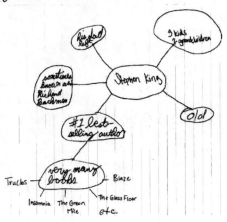

LESSON PLAN 8

LITERARY NEWS REPORT

WHAT *is a literary news report?*

A news article about an event or character in a book

WHY *engage students in this lesson?*

The lesson will help students:

- Capture the gist of a text in a summary.
- Judge and evaluate information critically.
- Negotiate an intended message and search for ways to record in a specific genre.

WHEN *might you use this lesson?*

Assessment analysis reveals that the student(s):

- Respond to text from one point of view.
- Display seemingly disconnected ideas and details in writing.

HOW *do you set up and use this lesson?*

Instructional steps:

1. Introduce multiple examples of real news reports to the students (newspapers, magazines, etc.).
2. Discuss the organization and writing format used in the examples. Note terms such as the *headline* (a short phase that catches the attention of the reader and provides an overview of what the report is about), *dateline* (information on where the story came from and when it was written), *slug line* (the first sentence of the report that extends on the headline), *body* (provides more details about who, what, when, where, why, and how. Quotations from the characters are usually included).
3. Present a folktale or fairy tale and show an example of a news report based on the story.

ASSESSMENT DIMENSIONS

Conversations/Inventories

Tools
- ⇨ Conversations
- ⇨ Surveys/Checklists
- ⇨ Observations

Link to Comprehending
- ○ Attitudes
- ○ Interests

Oral Reading

Tools
- ⇨ Running records
- ⇨ Miscue analysis
- ⇨ Informal reading inventory

Link to Comprehending
- ○ Decision making
- ○ Fluency

Constructing and Composing

Tools
- ⇨ Writing samples
- ⇨ Conversations

Link to Comprehending
- ○ Negotiating messages through text
- ○ Problem solving
- ○ Knowledge of letters and/or word patterns

Responding to Text

Tools
- ⇨ Conversations
- ⇨ Retelling
- ⇨ Oral and written and responses to open ended activities

Link to Comprehending
- ○ Analysis
- ○ Synthesis
- ○ Summarizing
- ○ Evaluating

59

4. Ask the student(s) to select another text to read. For younger students, read the text aloud. Older students will read the text independently. Instruct the student(s) to pay close attention, as they listen or read, to what happens to the main character(s) of the story.
5. Distribute materials. The student(s) will construct a literary news report.
6. Share reports with peers.

WHO *will benefit from this instruction, and how will you expect students to learn?*

Individual Instruction:

- Younger students may dictate what to write during one-to-one discussion of the text.
- Older students may engage in more in-depth analysis of the story elements of texts.

Small Group Instruction:

- Use reports to support guided reading or literature study groups.

Whole Class Instruction:

- Students may work collaboratively in small groups on the construction of one report or individual reports.

Bilingual Student(s) Instruction:

- Provide opportunities to use their first language to construct written responses.

Materials

A folk tale or fairy tale with a strong central character, example of a news report from the folktale or fairy tale, several nonfiction texts with a tight plot and characters (multiple copies if needed for instructional grouping), newspaper articles, paper, markers, and pencils.

Carolines Corner

Thursday May 20, 2004

George gains chompers!

By: Caroline Turner

George lozes his teeth!
This was a PROBLEM.
Because now he won't
eat AGIEN. The dentist
comes and makes fake
ones out of hippopotamus
tusks. Now he will eat
agin!

LITERARY NEWS REPORT
A THIRD GRADER'S WRITTEN RESPONSE

In my back yard
Back yard
May-20-2004

five days ago sixteen ants travold through
my Back yard up my house wall and
in to my Kichin. Thay skip into a bowl of
sweet shoger for my tee. Thay took it to
thar family. low ants travold in a world
of a hug bized. Thay thay finly got
home to thar family.

LITERARY REPORT CARD

WHAT *is a literary report card?*

A report card evaluating a character according to predetermined criteria

WHY *engage students in this lesson?*

The lesson will help students:

- Perceive reading and writing as enjoyable.
- Value their judgments related to character in order to establish a critical stance.
- Critically read in order to assign a value to a character's actions.
- Provide evidence for analysis and evaluative statements about characters.

WHEN *might you use this lesson?*

Assessment analysis reveals that the student(s):

- Only analyze characters minimally.

Response to text example:

> Student 1: "I think the pigs were brave."
> Student 2: "I don't know, maybe sometimes."
> Teacher: "Is there any time in the story when they were not brave?"

HOW *do you set up and use this lesson?*

Instructional steps:

1. Select several texts with strong characters of high interest to the student(s).
2. Engage student(s) in a discussion about report cards, using the terminology used by their school (e.g., grades, assessments, semester evaluations, grade reports, etc.).
3. Discuss the different subjects that are assessed and graded. Discuss what letter grades represent. Use a report card example if possible. If letter

ASSESSMENT DIMENSIONS

Conversations/Inventories
Tools
⇨ Conversations
⇨ Surveys/Checklists
⇨ Observations
Link to Comprehending
○ Attitudes
○ Interests

Oral Reading
Tools
⇨ Running records
⇨ Miscue analysis
⇨ Informal reading inventory
Link to Comprehending
○ Decision making
○ Fluency

Constructing and Composing
Tools
⇨ Writing samples
⇨ Conversations
Link to Comprehending
○ Negotiating messages through text
○ Problem solving
○ Knowledge of letters and/or word patterns

Responding to Text
Tools
⇨ Conversations
⇨ Retelling
⇨ Oral and written and responses to open ended activities
Link to Comprehending
○ Analysis
○ Synthesis
○ Summarizing
○ Evaluating

63

grades are not used in the school or at their grade level, frame the discussion around the form of reporting on progress used in the school district.

4. Present a partially completed literary report card example based on a character who is familiar to the students. Include all of the subject areas, but leave some of the grades incomplete. Examples of subject areas may include a full range of characteristics: honesty, cheerfulness, courage, and so on. Include comments section.

5. Engage the student(s) in discussion about the character.

6. Complete the literary report card example by assigning grades and including comments about why the grade was assigned to the character.

7. Students select a text for completing another literary report card. For younger students (K–1), demonstrate more and read aloud. Older students (grades 2–8) may self-select characters from chapter books.

8. Provide support for younger students in identifying subjects for grading from their comments.

9. Provide opportunities for students to share literary report cards with peers.

WHO *will benefit from this instruction, and how will you expect students to learn?*

Individual Instruction:

- The student may dictate what to write during a one-on-one discussion of the text.

Small Group Instruction:

- Students may construct a literary report card collaboratively in small groups.

Whole Class Instruction:

- Small groups select different characters in the same story.

Bilingual Student(s) Instruction:

- Use pictures and act out the various levels of "grading" for each "subject."

Materials

Texts with a strong central character and/or several other characters, partially completed example, paper, markers, and pencils.

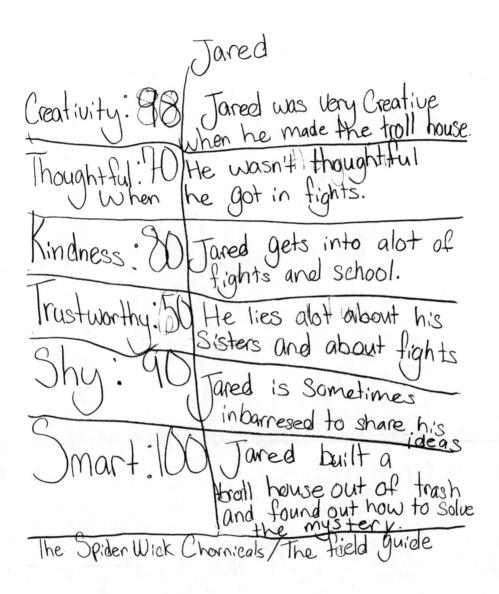

Jared

Creativity: 88 | Jared was very Creative when he made the troll house.

Thoughtful: 70 | He wasn't thoughtful when he got in fights.

Kindness: 80 | Jared gets into alot of fights and school.

Trustworthy: 50 | He lies alot about his Sisters and about fights

Shy: 90 | Jared is Sometimes inbarresed to share his ideas

Smart: 100 | Jared built a troll house out of trash and found out how to Solve the mystery.

The SpiderWick Chornicals / The field guide

LESSON PLAN 10

LITERARY SOCIOGRAM

WHAT *is a literary sociogram?*

An analysis of the relationships between text characters; how the characters feel about each other

WHY *engage students in this lesson?*

The lesson will help students:

- Identify relevant features of characters.
- Evaluate and infer relationships.

WHEN *might you use this lesson?*

Assessment analysis reveals that the student(s):

- Discuss texts by listing events without describing the relationships between key characters.
- Incorporate complex elements of characterization in writing.

A student's written retelling:

- There were pigs.
- The pigs built houses.
- The wolf tore them down.
- The pigs tricked the wolf.
- The pigs were safe.

HOW *do you set up and use this lesson?*

Instructional steps:

1. Share an example of a literary sociogram, discussing the organization, identifying the characters, feelings, and how the use of arrows can be used to show the relationships among the text characters.
2. Ask the student(s) to select a text for developing a literary sociogram. For younger readers, read the selected text aloud. Older readers may read the text independently.

Conversations/Inventories
Tools
- ⇨ Conversations
- ⇨ Surveys/Checklists
- ⇨ Observations

Link to Comprehending
- ○ Attitudes
- ○ Interests

Oral Reading
Tools
- ⇨ Running records
- ⇨ Miscue analysis
- ⇨ Informal reading inventory

Link to Comprehending
- ○ Decision making
- ○ Fluency

Constructing and Composing
Tools
- ⇨ Writing samples
- ⇨ Conversations

Link to Comprehending
- ○ Negotiating messages through text
- ○ Problem solving
- ○ Knowledge of letters and/or word patterns

Responding to Text
Tools
- ⇨ Conversations
- ⇨ Retelling
- ⇨ Oral and written and responses to open ended activities

Link to Comprehending
- ○ Analysis
- ○ Synthesis
- ○ Summarizing
- ○ Evaluating

67

3. Discuss the students' feelings about the characters and the characters' feelings for each other.
4. On a sheet of paper, have the students place a circle(s) near the center of the paper and write the name(s) of the central character(s).
5. Discuss how the placement of the other character's circles, or size of circles, might show the relationship of the characters to one another (e.g., a student might be placed closer to a parent, and a neighbor might be placed further from the central character, etc.). Draw arrows to show the direction of the character's relationships (love, jealousy) to other characters.
6. Encourage experimentation with different ways of showing relationships (e.g., broken arrow lines vs. solid arrow lines).
7. Share literary sociogram with peers.

WHO will benefit from this instruction, and how will you expect students to learn?

Individual Instruction:

- Share responsibility and scaffold the writing and graphic organization.

Small Group Instruction:

- Provide support to guided reading or literature study small groups.

Whole Class Instruction:

- Model the construction of a literary sociogram to the whole class.

Bilingual Student(s) Instruction:

- Provide many examples of texts portraying characters that the students can relate to linguistically and culturally.

Materials

Several examples of fiction or biographical texts with a strong central character and several other characters (multiple copies if needed for instructional grouping), paper, markers, and pencils.

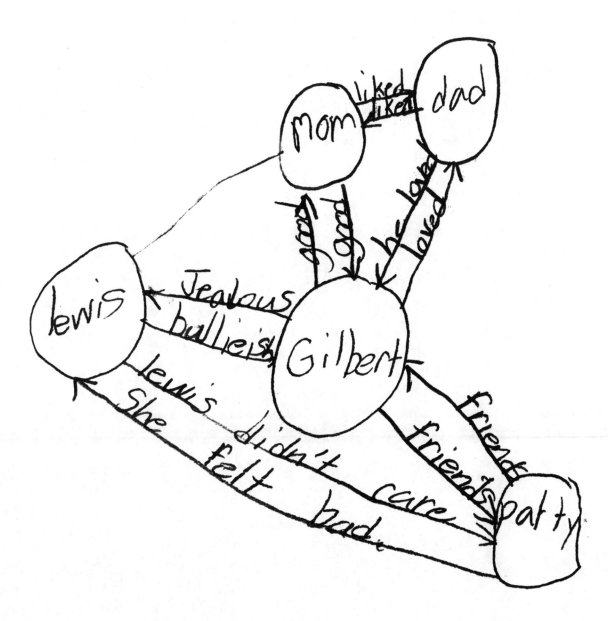

LITERARY TALK SHOW

WHAT *is a literary talk show?*

A preplanned interview of characters or a historical figure role-played by students; students write questions and potential responses taking the perspective of the interviewer or interviewee

WHY *engage students in this lesson?*

The lesson will help students:

- Understand the power of literacy not only in the classroom but also in the real world.
- Negotiate and compose questions.
- Understand multiple perspectives.

WHEN *might you use this lesson?*

Assessment analysis reveals that the student(s):

- Need support constructing a positive literate identity.

Writing Examples

- A student writing a response to reading looks for an "answer" in the text. Little evidence of negotiating a written message.

HOW *do you set up and use this lesson?*

Instructional steps:

1. Select a text with multiple characters that students find interesting.
2. Discuss how talk-show hosts (like Oprah Winfrey) prepare for interviews. For example, they gather background knowledge by reading about the guest and/or talking to other people about the guest.
3. Explain that students will work in pairs. One person will be the talk-show host and one will play the character in the text.
4. Read the text aloud.

ASSESSMENT DIMENSIONS

Conversations/Inventories
Tools
⇨ Conversations
⇨ Surveys/Checklists
⇨ Observations
Link to Comprehending
o Attitudes
o Interests

Oral Reading
Tools
⇨ Running records
⇨ Miscue analysis
⇨ Informal reading inventory
Link to Comprehending
o Decision making
o Fluency

Constructing and Composing
Tools
⇨ Writing samples
⇨ Conversations
Link to Comprehending
o Negotiating messages through text
o Problem solving
o Knowledge of letters and/or word patterns

Responding to Text
Tools
⇨ Conversations
⇨ Retelling
⇨ Oral and written and responses to open ended activities
Link to Comprehending
o Analysis
o Synthesis
o Summarizing
o Evaluating

71

5. Demonstrate how to write open-ended questions. What would viewers (readers) want to know about the character? What is interesting? What does the character plan to do in the future? For example, "Why did you decide to go home and leave the wild rumpus? What did your mom say to you when you returned? Will you ever go back to where the wild things are?"
6. Explain how talk-show hosts encourage guests to talk, discussing body language and nonverbal communication. Carefully crafted questions probe or generate more in-depth responses. Generate questions and a plan for presentation.
7. Take turns role-playing the talk-show host and the guest roles.
8. After the talk show, discuss what the student(s) learned about interviews and characters. In the future, students may elect to videotape talk shows for sharing. In addition, one host could interview multiple characters at the same time (e.g., Cinderella and her stepsisters).

WHO *will benefit from this instruction, and how will you expect students to learn?*

Individual Instruction:

- Teachers may take the role of talk-show host and students answer questions.

Small Group Instruction:

- Small groups "produce" an interview taking different roles: writer, director, talk-show host, interviewee.

Whole Class Instruction:

- Demonstrate with a character, and have students select another in the same text.

Bilingual Student(s) Instruction:

- Support writing questions through partnering students.
- Students may dictate the questions and the teacher records them.

Materials

Fiction or nonfiction text with multidimensional characters (multiple copies for small group/whole class instruction), and pens or markers.

wiy DID You go wi
the wiallD thagz?
wiy DiD You lefo?
wiy DiD You geti
tro Ball?
are You go weN
Back?
wiy DiD treso growiN
Yor rom?

LESSON PLAN 12

MAIN IDEA MAP

WHAT *is a main idea map?*

A visual analysis and synthesis of the relationships between the central thought or message of text and supporting details

WHY *engage students in this lesson?*

The lesson will help students:

- Analyze explicit and implicit central ideas of paragraphs or text-level messages.
- Synthesize details to support the proposed central idea of the text.

WHEN *might you use this lesson?*

Assessment analysis reveals that the student(s):

- Talk about unimportant features of an informational text.
- Incorporate some critical features of fiction writing.
- Read texts that seem "just right," and emphasis on conceptual organization would be appropriate.
- Write, "Ladybugs are insects. Spiders have eight legs. I think ladybugs bite people. Flies get in food."

HOW *do you set up and use this lesson?*

Instructional steps:

1. Select one expository or nonfiction text that has one clear main idea for the passages and the text.
2. Write the title of the text on the main idea map.
3. Read the text to the student(s). For younger students (grades K–2), read the text aloud. For older students (grades 3–8), read the text aloud or provide multiple copies for independent reading.
4. Engage the students in a discussion about what they think are the most important messages in the text.

5. Write the main idea on the graphic organizer.
6. Reread the text to the students, stopping at each passage that has a clear main idea.
7. Engage students in a discussion about the main idea of each passage.
8. Record the passage's main ideas on the graphic organizer.
9. Ask the students to select a new text to read. Engage them in discussion about elements of the text that are key when selecting the texts. Make sure they are selecting texts that have clear passages and text main ideas.
10. Have students work collaboratively to identify the main idea of the passages and the text. They will complete a main idea map.
11. Each group or individual will share his or her completed main idea map as appropriate.

WHO *will benefit from this instruction, and how will you expect students to learn?*

Individual Instruction:

- Scaffold the synthesis through questioning.

Small Group Instruction:

- Complete a main idea map for different historical characters based on interests.

Whole Class Instruction:

- Small groups complete main idea maps for different texts.

Bilingual Student(s) Instruction:

- Provide opportunities for extended conversations around central idea.
- Act out the central idea.

Materials

Texts with clear passages and text main ideas (one for demonstration, multiple copies for independent work), a main idea map large enough for group demonstration, and 8½ × 11 main idea maps (one per group or one per student).

MAIN IDEA MAP
A FIFTH GRADER'S WRITTEN RESPONSE

Two Bad Ants – Chris Van Allsburg   Name _____

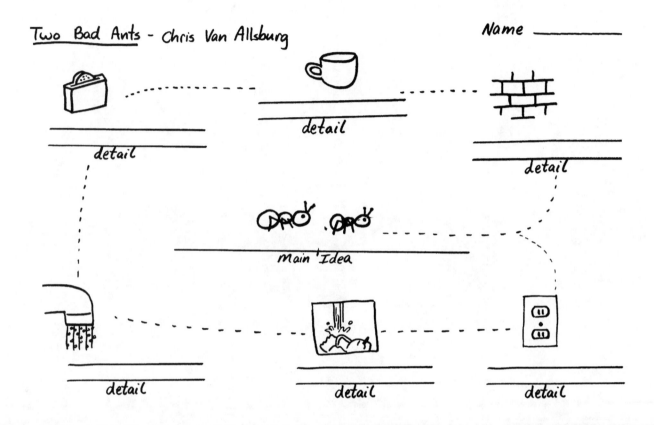

_____
detail

_____
detail

_____
detail

_____
Main Idea

_____
detail

_____
detail

_____
detail

LESSON PLAN 13

OPEN AND CLOSED SORT

WHAT *is an open and closed sort?*

A list of words arranged in groups by students according to relationships; closed sorts include predetermined group labels, and open sorts do not

WHY *engage students in this lesson?*

The lesson will help students:

- Synthesize information from the text.
- Explain and visualize relationships.
- Draw conclusions based on relevant information.
- Negotiate relationships via conversations with other students and teachers.

WHEN *might you use this lesson?*

Assessment analysis reveals that the student(s):

- Need to attend to patterns in words.
- Converse around new concepts in minimal ways.
- While reading a book about snakes, students may not connect what they already know to specific facts (e.g., snakes lay eggs and are reptiles).

HOW *do you set up and use this lesson?*

Instructional steps:

1. Select an informational nonfiction text and identify 10 to 20 key concepts. Make sure to include some concepts the students will know. Write the words on cards in large print. Make enough sets of words for small groups to work with an entire set.
2. Predetermine the categories for the words. For a closed sort, provide a card with the labels for each category. For an open sort, provide blank cards for the students to generate the labels for each category.

ASSESSMENT DIMENSIONS

Conversations/Inventories
Tools
⇨ Conversations
⇨ Surveys/Checklists
⇨ Observations
Link to Comprehending
○ Attitudes
○ Interests

Oral Reading
Tools
⇨ Running records
⇨ Miscue analysis
⇨ Informal reading inventory
Link to Comprehending
○ Decision making
○ Fluency

Constructing and Composing
Tools
⇨ Writing samples
⇨ Conversations
Link to Comprehending
○ Negotiating messages through text
○ Problem solving
○ Knowledge of letters and/or word patterns

Responding to Text
Tools
⇨ Conversations
⇨ Retelling
⇨ Oral and written and responses to open ended activities
Link to Comprehending
○ Analysis
○ Synthesis
○ Summarizing
○ Evaluating

3. Introduce the topic and generate conversation.
4. Demonstrate and think aloud, grouping words into one category, and then ask the students to find another category.
5. After students complete grouping, share and compare, encouraging students to listen and confirm or refine categories.
6. Read the text aloud.
7. After reading, ask students to refine categories and discuss the common features of the meanings.

WHO *will benefit from this instruction, and how will you expect students to learn?*

Individual Instruction:

- Students who have particular needs related to understanding letters/ sounds/word patterns would benefit from selecting based on spelling patterns.

Small Group Instruction:

- Design different sorts based on flexible groups of identified needs.

Whole Class Instruction:

- In content areas, such as science and social studies, word sorts help the entire class engage in conversation around texts, thus supporting comprehension.

Bilingual Student(s) Instruction:

- Incorporate pictures to help the sorting and encourage discussion.

Materials

Texts around the nonfiction topic (multiple copies for small group/whole class instruction), and words on cards in sets for group work.

OPEN AND CLOSED SORT
TWO SIXTH GRADERS' WRITTEN RESPONSES

Sliding plates	After Shock
Faults	California
Magma	Lava
Mountains	Japan
North Pacific	Paohoehoe
Hawaii	ah-ah
Mt . St. Helens	Richter scale

These words are about Volcanoes & Earthquakes:

-seven words will go under each heading

Volcanoes	*Earthquakes*
1. Magma	1. Sliding Plates
2. Hawaii	2. Faults
3. Mountains	3. North Pacific
4. Mt. St. Helens	4. After Shock
5. Lava	5. California
6. Pahoehoe	6. Japan
7. Ah-ah	7. Richter scale

Tornadoes	Lightning
Cyclones	Bolts
Dust Devil	Electricity
Fujita-Pearson Intensity Scale	Ice Crystals
Spring	Stepped Leaders
Funnel	Fulgurite
Tornada	Sprites
Water Spouts	Sheets

READERS' THEATER

WHAT *is readers' theater?*

Students write a script and represent the text dramatically.

WHY *engage students in this lesson?*

The lesson will help students:

- Develop a positive literate identity.
- Read fluently.
- Summarize text and negotiate a message to perform.

WHEN *might you use this lesson?*

Assessment analysis reveals that the student(s):

- Read slowly, word by word.
- Summarize texts in very literal ways.
- Interact productively in relation to the text more when working with other student(s).

Oral reading example:

"The Three Little Pigs"

Text: "The little pig said, 'Not by the hair of my chinney chin chin.'"
Student: "The (pause) little (pause) pig (pause) said, (pause) "'Not (pause) by (pause) the hair (pause) of my (pause) chinney chin chin.'"

HOW *do you set up and use this lesson?*

Instructional steps:

1. Select several high-interest texts with clear and lively plots.
2. Engage student(s) in a discussion about drama, theater, and movies, focusing on how to turn a text into a drama.

ASSESSMENT DIMENSIONS

Conversations/Inventories
Tools
- ⇨ Conversations
- ⇨ Surveys/Checklists
- ⇨ Observations

Link to Comprehending
- ○ Attitudes
- ○ Interests

Oral Reading
Tools
- ⇨ Running records
- ⇨ Miscue analysis
- ⇨ Informal reading inventory

Link to Comprehending
- ○ Decision making
- ○ Fluency

Constructing and Composing
Tools
- ⇨ Writing samples
- ⇨ Conversations

Link to Comprehending
- ○ Negotiating messages through text
- ○ Problem solving
- ○ Knowledge of letters and/or word patterns

Responding to Text
Tools
- ⇨ Conversations
- ⇨ Retelling
- ⇨ Oral and written and responses to open ended activities

Link to Comprehending
- ○ Analysis
- ○ Synthesis
- ○ Summarizing
- ○ Evaluating

3. Share an example of a script made for the text (developed for this lesson or published). Introduce use of a narrator for communicating essential plot, setting, background details, and so on, to the audience.
4. Discuss elements of the text key to dramatization (characters, plot, theme, and setting).
5. Guide the students through a prewritten example demonstrating staging and potential use of props.
6. Student(s) develop a script with props, puppets, costumes, and so on, as time permits. List the characters' names, including the narrator, on the left side of the chart paper, noting what each will say. Plan and develop sound effects, props, and puppets as needed.
7. Copy the script for all participants.
8. Have students determine staging and practice.
9. Perform the script for peers.

WHO *will benefit from this instruction, and how will you expect students to learn?*

Individual Instruction:

- Share the writing of the script with two characters and perform with the student.

Small Group Instruction:

- Small groups may select different texts or portions of a chapter book.

Whole Class Instruction:

- Students may develop different scripts for the same story and share and compare the differences and similarities.

Bilingual Student(s) Instruction:

- Students may need to begin with the "acting" portion and the teacher takes dictation from their oral language, scaffolding the creation of the script.

Materials

Texts for introduction and development of a script, an example of an original or published script, chart paper, pens or markers, props, costumes, puppets, and so on, as needed.

Wolf: This is a story about three pigs but in my way. this whole story is a misunder standing. you can help me clear it up. maby if you tell people about THIS way people will know it the right way.

Wolf: I am going to tell you the real story. See I had a cold and I was making a cake for my granny. and I ran out of shuger. and so I went to my next door nighbor. He was a pig. That was a problem. So I knocked on the door and no anwser. So I called Little pig little pig let me come in *narriaP knock knock*

Pig: NO Way!

Wolf: How rude!

Wolf: so I went to the 1st pigs brother

Narirator: Knock knock

Pig: Whos there?
Wolf: wolf
Pig: wolf who?
Wolf: Alexzander T. wolf
Pig: You cant come in!

Mead

85

LESSON PLAN  15

SHARED WRITING

WHAT *is shared writing?*

Students and teachers share responsibility, negotiate, and record a self-selected or predetermined message; teachers scaffold and support specific aspects of responding and comprehending.

WHY *engage students in this lesson?*

The lesson will help students:

- Apply knowledge of how to construct messages and develop letter and/or patterns in words.
- Understand how to negotiate a message and problem-solve ways of recording.

WHEN *might you use this lesson?*

Assessment analysis reveals that the student(s):

- Need support composing or are reluctant to write.
- Demonstrate an emerging knowledge of problem-solving patterns in words.
- Illustrate in their writing an understanding of a consonant framework (e.g., CT for cat or DG for dog).
- Stop at words when writing independently and appeal to the teacher for help.

HOW *do you set up and use this lesson?*

Instructional steps:

1. Determine if the topic and genre will be self-selected by the student or predetermined by the teacher.
2. Engage student(s) in a discussion about the topic selected. Support and list the student's ideas as he or she brainstorms.
3. After the brainstorming session is exhausted, work together in sequencing the story.

Conversations/Inventories
Tools
⇨ Conversations
⇨ Surveys/Checklists
⇨ Observations
Link to Comprehending
○ Attitudes
○ Interests

Oral Reading
Tools
⇨ Running records
⇨ Miscue analysis
⇨ Informal reading
   inventory
Link to Comprehending
○ Decision making
○ Fluency

Constructing and Composing
Tools
⇨ Writing samples
⇨ Conversations
Link to Comprehending
○ Negotiating messages
   through text
○ Problem solving
○ Knowledge of letters
   and/or word patterns

Responding to Text
Tools
⇨ Conversations
⇨ Retelling
⇨ Oral and written and
   responses to open
   ended activities
Link to Comprehending
○ Analysis
○ Synthesis
○ Summarizing
○ Evaluating

4. Work together in developing paragraphs. This includes working on the sentences within each paragraph.
5. Record the story or information as it develops. If constructing a book, decide on the placement of the page breaks.
6. If necessary, go back to revise and edit the shared writing to make a final product.
7. Publish the writing in its final form (chart, big book, small book, newspaper, etc.).
8. Read the final product and then place it in an appropriate place where students can read it during independent reading time.

WHO *will benefit from this instruction, and how will you expect students to learn?*

Individual Instruction:

- Carefully examine the student's writing for strengths to build on and areas of growth. Support the student in the areas of growth and take responsibility for aspects of composing and recording that are not yet independent.

Small Group Instruction:

- Students construct a story or informational text in a small group with the teacher scaffolding the students.

Whole Class Instruction:

- Select an aspect of writing to focus the lesson, and think aloud the process of composing and problem solving.

Bilingual Student(s) Instruction:

- Provide extended time for oral language development and negotiating a message. Illustrations may support initial composing.

Materials

Paper necessary to complete the shared writing (e.g., chart paper, multiple paper if constructing a book), marker dark enough and with a wide enough tip to be viewed by all participants, and Post-it tape.

SKETCH-TO-STRETCH

WHAT *is sketch-to-stretch?*

A visual representation students draw of the unique meanings constructed of text

WHY *engage students in this lesson?*

The lesson will help students:

- Respond artistically and see reading/writing as enjoyable literacy events.
- Evaluate information in order to take a critical stance toward the text.

WHEN *might you use this lesson?*

Assessment analysis reveals that the student(s):

- Discuss literal interpretations of texts.
- Reflect a negative view of literacy via their responses to the text.
- Make negative comments about reading and writing.
- Show strengths in the area of artistic representation.

HOW *do you set up and use this lesson?*

Instructional steps:

1. Select several expository or fiction texts of high interest to the students.
2. Before reading the text, ask the students to consider, "What does the text mean to you?" Distribute materials for sketching.
3. Students select one text to read. For younger students, read the text aloud. Older students may read the text independently.
4. Encourage students to explore, extend, express, and share interpretations of expository and/or fiction texts without judging artistic qualities.
5. Encourage students to experiment, focusing on interpretation rather than on the artistic qualities.
6. Comment that there are many ways to sketch what a text means to us.
7. Provide an opportunity for students to share sketches with peers.

ASSESSMENT DIMENSIONS

Conversations/Inventories
Tools
- ⇨ Conversations
- ⇨ Surveys/Checklists
- ⇨ Observations

Link to Comprehending
- ○ Attitudes
- ○ Interests

Oral Reading
Tools
- ⇨ Running records
- ⇨ Miscue analysis
- ⇨ Informal reading inventory

Link to Comprehending
- ○ Decision making
- ○ Fluency

Constructing and Composing
Tools
- ⇨ Writing samples
- ⇨ Conversations

Link to Comprehending
- ○ Negotiating messages through text
- ○ Problem solving
- ○ Knowledge of letters and/or word patterns

Responding to Text
Tools
- ⇨ Conversations
- ⇨ Retelling
- ⇨ Oral and written and responses to open ended activities

Link to Comprehending
- ○ Analysis
- ○ Synthesis
- ○ Summarizing
- ○ Evaluating

89

WHO *will benefit from this instruction, and how will you expect students to learn?*

Individual Instruction:

- To facilitate more discussion, read the text aloud. Both the teacher and the student will sketch responses to the text reading.

Small Group Instruction:

- Use sketch-to-stretch during flexible grouping as a response to a small group reading lesson.

Whole Class Instruction:

- Students may listen to one oral text reading, sketch responses, and discuss sketches as a whole class.

Bilingual Student(s) Instruction:

- Encourage children to engage in conversations around their illustrations to extend oral language development.

Materials

Several fiction and/or nonfiction texts, art materials: colored paper, markers, colored pencils, watercolors, and so on.

PeNDragon

The Lost City of Faar

91

STORY MAP

WHAT *is a story map?*

A visual representation of the critical features of problem- or goal-centered text

WHY *engage students in this lesson?*

The lesson will help students:

- Analyze the critical features of story structure (e.g., characters, setting, plot).
- Monitor comprehension in order to search for meaning while reading texts.
- Plan writing in order to compose text including critical features of a story.

WHEN *might you use this lesson?*

Assessment analysis reveals that the student(s):

- Respond literally to text, or in "creative" ways.
- Notice literary elements (e.g., characters, setting, beginning, middle, and ending).

Response to text example:

"The Three Little Pigs"

Student: "There were three pigs and a wolf. He wanted to eat 'em."
Student: "It was made of sticks."
Student: "The wolf was hairy."

HOW *do you set up and use this lesson?*

Instructional steps:

1. Select two texts with a clear problem and solution.
2. Read aloud the first text. Present and discuss parts of the story map and relate them to story elements (e.g., characters, setting, problem/goal, events, solution).

ASSESSMENT DIMENSIONS

Conversations/Inventories

Tools
- ⇨ Conversations
- ⇨ Surveys/Checklists
- ⇨ Observations

Link to Comprehending
- ○ Attitudes
- ○ Interests

Oral Reading

Tools
- ⇨ Running records
- ⇨ Miscue analysis
- ⇨ Informal reading inventory

Link to Comprehending
- ○ Decision making
- ○ Fluency

Constructing and Composing

Tools
- ⇨ Writing samples
- ⇨ Conversations

Link to Comprehending
- ○ Negotiating messages through text
- ○ Problem solving
- ○ Knowledge of letters and/or word patterns

Responding to Text

Tools
- ⇨ Conversations
- ⇨ Retelling
- ⇨ Oral and written and responses to open ended activities

Link to Comprehending
- ○ Analysis
- ○ Synthesis
- ○ Summarizing
- ○ Evaluating

93

Figure III.3 Story Map Form

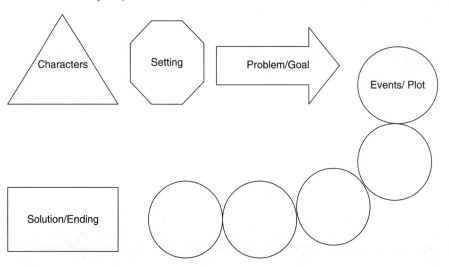

3. Demonstrate how to complete a story map, using chart paper or overhead projector.
4. Read aloud the second book.
5. Provide students with a story map form (see figure III.3) and a copy of the book.
6. Students will construct / write story map.
7. Share and compare story maps.

WHO *will benefit from this instruction, and how will you expect students to learn?*

Individual Instruction:

- The student may dictate what to write during a one-on-one discussion of the text.

Small Group Instruction:

- Literature study groups may construct a story map collaboratively.

Whole Class Instruction:

- Clear demonstrations provide the foundation for later independent analysis of texts, including chapter books with older students.

Bilingual Student(s) Instruction:

- Use pictures initially to illustrate literary elements and engage in discussion and/or active engagement of acting out the plot as it is recorded.

Materials

Two texts with multiple copies, pens or markers, and copies of story map form.

STORY MAP
A FIRST GRADER'S WRITTEN RESPONSE

Story Map

Title: Walter the Baker

Author: Eric Carle

Characters
Walter
Duke   Walter Jr.
Duchess Anna

Setting
Bakarey
Casol
Duchy

Problem/Goal
He ran out of milk
Make a spestol roll

Events/Plot
His wife Anna allwase sold his rolls

Walter Jr. went to the Casol to give the Duke and Duchess a roll every morning

Walter ran out of milk for the Duke and Duchess.

He used water for the Duke and Duchess

The Duke told Walter to invint a new roll that was good

Solution/Ending
He akadintly made a prezel his new invitin and the Duke liked it.

STORY MAP
A SECOND GRADER'S WRITTEN RESPONSE

Lyndsey

Story Map

Title: Miss Nelson is Missing

Author: James Marshall

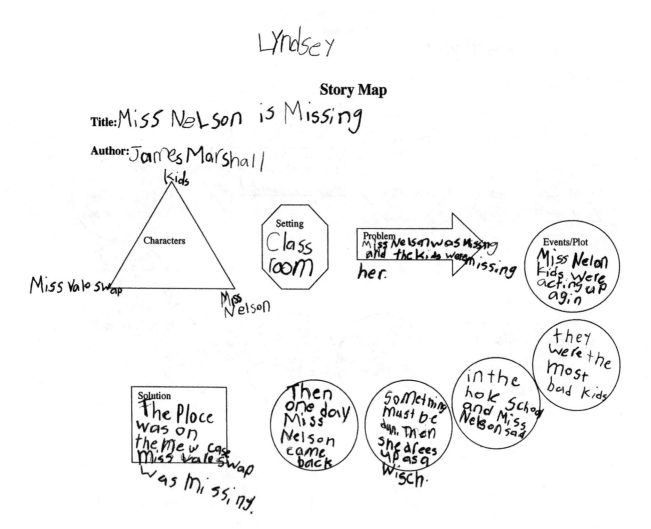

Characters (triangle):
Kids
Miss Valo swap
Miss Nelson

Setting (octagon):
Class room

Problem (arrow):
Miss Nelson was missing and the kids were missing her.

Events/Plot (circles):
Miss Nelon kids were acting up agin

they were the most bad kids

in the hole School and Miss Nelson sad

Something must be dun. Then she drees up as a Wisch.

Then one day Miss Nelson came back

Solution (box):
The Ploce was on the mew case Miss vale swap was Missing.

LESSON PLAN 18

SUMMARY PYRAMID

WHAT *is a summary pyramid?*

A summary of text represented by words arranged in a pyramid

WHY *engage students in this lesson?*

The lesson will help students:

- Evaluate information in text.
- Combine information to make inferences.
- Include significant information in summaries.

WHEN *might you use this lesson?*

Assessment analysis reveals that the student(s):

- Evaluate ideas in ways that focus on small details.
- Summarize text with difficulty.
- Retell stories with what seems to be lack of understanding.
- Write with lack of cohesion.

Response to text example:

A student who is asked to summarize "The Three Little Pigs" may say, "The wolf was bad, " which does not encompass the entire story into a synthesis.

HOW *do you set up and use this lesson?*

Instructional steps:

1. Select two high-interest or curriculum-based texts that support summarization.
2. Define summarization and provide a rationale for why it is a relevant literacy practice.
3. Show a pyramid summary form. The lines may be adapted to predetermine elements to be included in the summary or it may be left open.

ASSESSMENT DIMENSIONS

Conversations/Inventories
Tools
- ⇨ Conversations
- ⇨ Surveys/Checklists
- ⇨ Observations

Link to Comprehending
- ○ Attitudes
- ○ Interests

Oral Reading
Tools
- ⇨ Running records
- ⇨ Miscue analysis
- ⇨ Informal reading inventory

Link to Comprehending
- ○ Decision making
- ○ Fluency

Constructing and Composing
Tools
- ⇨ Writing samples
- ⇨ Conversations

Link to Comprehending
- ○ Negotiating messages through text
- ○ Problem solving
- ○ Knowledge of letters and/or word patterns

Responding to Text
Tools
- ⇨ Conversations
- ⇨ Retelling
- ⇨ Oral and written and responses to open ended activities

Link to Comprehending
- ○ Analysis
- ○ Synthesis
- ○ Summarizing
- ○ Evaluating

4. Read the first text. Think aloud and determine critical words or concepts.
5. Demonstrate how to fill in the pyramid summary. Students must decide on one, two, three, four, or five key words to fill in the lines.
6. Read the second text. Ask students to listen and take notes for critical words or concepts.
7. Ask students to fill out a second pyramid summary individually or in groups.
8. Have students share and compare pyramid summaries.

WHO *will benefit from this instruction, and how will you expect students to learn?*

Individual Instruction:

- Support students' initial summary by preselecting words or concepts they may pick from to arrange on the pyramid.

Small Group Instruction:

- Groups work cooperatively and make decisions about key words and the summary statement.

Whole Class Instruction:

- Demonstrate with a short nonfiction article. Then let students select individual articles to summarize.

Bilingual Student(s) Instruction:

- Provide extra conversational, descriptive support.
- Allow students to draw and talk about the concepts selected.

Materials

Two short texts appropriate for learning how to summarize, blank pyramid forms, and markers.

SUMMARY PYRAMID
TWO SIXTH GRADERS' WRITTEN RESPONSES

Name: Mary Schwartzkopf
Name of Book: Radio Rescue
Author: Lynne Barasch

Pyramid Poem

boy
Who

Morris code   radio transmittions
What

apartment   1926 (past)   summer
Where and When

communication   rescue   long-distance   getting licensed
                          communication
Why

Summary: Boy from past, 1926, one summer resued family through morris code communication with radio transmittor.

99

Name: Pablo d. Salazr
Name of Book: The true Story of three litle Pigs
Author: Jon scleszka

Pyramid Poem

Wolf
Who

coln   cup of sugar
What

cun fly   Pigs hose   once apon
Where and When   a time

Gany b, day   mean pig   trure story   primed
Why

Summary: Wolf was framed he tou true story

100

LESSON PLAN 19

VENN DIAGRAM

WHAT *is a Venn diagram?*

A visual representation of how two texts, characters, or other literacy elements are similar and different in two overlapping circles

WHY *engage students in this lesson?*

The lesson will help students:

- Determine, evaluate, and analyze critical features of text.
- Monitor comprehension of text read silently or aloud.

WHEN *might you use this lesson?*

Assessment analysis reveals that the student(s):

- Write expository texts listing ideas without comparative analysis.
- Respond in a linear fashion, without linking or comparing literary elements or ideas across texts.

Response to text example:

Teacher: How are Thomas Jefferson and George Washington similar?
What characteristics do they share?
Student 1: They are both men.
Student 2: I don't know.

HOW *do you set up and use this lesson?*

Instructional steps:

1. Select two texts with several common characteristics or features. This lesson may compare characters in a story or historical figures in nonfiction.
2. Read both texts to the student(s). Discuss common attributes and characteristics (things, places, events, ideas, people, information).
3. Share and discuss an example of a common characteristic or attribute.
4. Demonstrate placement of characteristics that are unique to text A and B.

ASSESSMENT DIMENSIONS

Conversations/Inventories
Tools
  ⇨ Conversations
  ⇨ Surveys/Checklists
  ⇨ Observations
Link to Comprehending
  ○ Attitudes
  ○ Interests

Oral Reading
Tools
  ⇨ Running records
  ⇨ Miscue analysis
  ⇨ Informal reading inventory
Link to Comprehending
  ○ Decision making
  ○ Fluency

Constructing and Composing
Tools
  ⇨ Writing samples
  ⇨ Conversations
Link to Comprehending
  ○ Negotiating messages through text
  ○ Problem solving
  ○ Knowledge of letters and/or word patterns

Responding to Text
Tools
  ⇨ Conversations
  ⇨ Retelling
  ⇨ Oral and written and responses to open ended activities
Link to Comprehending
  ○ Analysis
  ○ Synthesis
  ○ Summarizing
  ○ Evaluating

101

5. Have students work collaboratively to name more common and unique characteristics and attributes.
6. Ask each group or individual to share his or her completed Venn diagram.

WHO *will benefit from this instruction, and how will you expect students to learn?*

Individual Instruction:

- The student may dictate what to write during one-on-one discussion of the text.

Small Group Instruction:

- Small groups may select different versions of fairy tales to compare. For example, there are at least four cultural versions of Cinderella. They may select two of the four to compare and contrast.

Whole Class Instruction:

- Students may work collaboratively in small groups to construct a Venn diagram. Small groups may present to the entire class.

Bilingual Student(s) Instruction:

- Provide student(s) with objects to use in the Venn diagram before using texts (e.g., sort unique and common characteristics of rocks).

Materials

Texts with unique and common characteristics or attributes. Chart paper with a Venn diagram for demonstration and copies for each student.

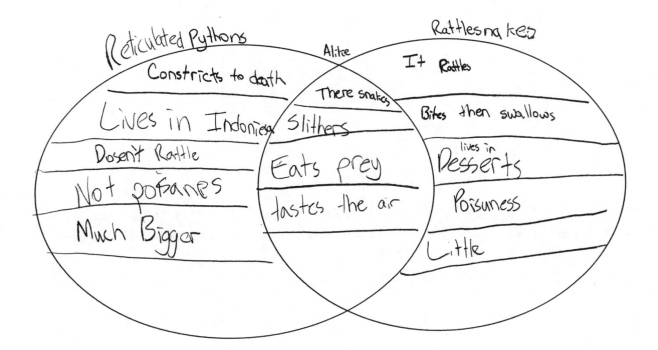

Reticulated Pythons

Constricts to death

Lives in Indoniea

Dosen't Rattle

Not poisanes

Much Bigger

Alike

There snakes

Slithers

Eats prey

tastes the air

Rattlesnakes

It Rattles

Bites then swallows

lives in
Desserts

Poisuness

Little

LESSON PLAN

VOCABULARY WEB

WHAT *is a vocabulary web?*

A visual representation resembling a web of concepts and subordinating ideas arranged with connecting lines to show relationships

WHY *engage students in this lesson?*

The lesson will help students:

- Synthesize by connecting information.
- Pull together relevant information.
- Explore vocabulary text read in order to monitor and self-correct for meaning.

WHEN *might you use this lesson?*

Assessment analysis reveals that the student(s):

- Retell text in meager ways because of lack of understanding related to vocabulary.
- Write with great redundancy, overusing specific words.

Writing example:

> In a composed story, the student writes, "She was nice and good. She liked everyone. She had lots of friends."

HOW *do you set up and use this lesson?*

Instructional steps:

1. Select a text with rich vocabulary.
2. Read the text to the student(s).
3. Select one unknown vocabulary word and write it in the circle on the web.
4. Demonstrate and discuss how to write a sentence containing the vocabulary word in the triangle.
5. Use a developmentally appropriate dictionary or electronic dictionary to locate the formal definition.

105

6. In the oval, write the definition. If there are multiple definitions, use only the definition that relates to the text sentence.
7. Discuss, identify, and write synonyms for the word in the parallelogram.
8. Discuss and compose a new sentence using the vocabulary word and record on the rectangle.
9. Have students select another word from the same text to complete another web collaboratively. Emphasize independent identification of new words/concepts to learn.

WHO will benefit from this instruction, and how will you expect students to learn?

Individual Instruction:

- Demonstrate further how to select words and complete multiple webs with an individual.

Small Group Instruction:

- Demonstrate the use of a vocabulary web when new words are found during shared or guided reading or writing.

Whole Class Instruction:

- Demonstrate the use of a vocabulary web when new words are found during a read-aloud and shared reading/writing.

Bilingual Student(s) Instruction:

- Begin with words that can be represented by objects.
- Use a word from a student's first language to build a vocabulary web. For example, use the word *gato* instead of cat. Then complete the vocabulary web as directed.

Materials

Texts with unique vocabulary words, chart paper with a large web, blank webs for each student or the students may draw the webs from the example.

VOCABULARY WEB
A SIXTH GRADER'S WRITTEN RESPONSE

The View From Saturday

What does paraplegic mean?

Definition: paralysis of both lower limbs due to spinal disease or injury.

Synonyms: Google dictionary didn't have any synonyms. I came up with these synonyms from an old dictionary— paralyzed, paralytic.

Sentence: The woman was paraplegic and couldn't move both of her arms and legs.

What does Theatrical mean?

Definition: of or pertaining to the theater or dramatic presentations

Synonyms: Drama, dramatic, extravagant, flashy, thespian, stagy, playwriting.

Sentence: One of the most popular theatrical elements is playwriting.

What does Chanteuse mean?

Definition: a female singer, esp. one who sings in nightclubs and cabarets.

Sentence: In the Phantom of the Opera there was an excellent chanteuse.

REFERENCES

Allard, H., & Marshall, J. (1985). *Miss Nelson is missing!* Boston: Houghton Mifflin.

Allard, H., Marshall, J., & Canetti, Y. (1998). *¡La señorita Nelson ha desparecido!* Boston: Houghton Mifflin.

Allington, R. L. (2006). *What really matters for struggling readers: Designing research-based programs* (2nd ed.). Boston: Pearson/Allyn & Bacon.

Baehr, P. (2002). *For a good cause.* New York: Newbridge.

Barasch, L. (2000). *Radio rescue* (1st ed.). New York: Frances Foster Books.

Barton, D. (1994). *Literacy: An introduction to the ecology of written language.* Cambridge, MA: Blackwell.

Barton, D., & Hamilton, M. (1998). *Local literacies: Reading and writing in one community.* New York: Routledge.

Beaver, J., & Carter, M. (2006). *Developmental reading assessment* (DRA2) (2nd ed.). Columbus: Celebration Press/Pearson Learning Group.

Black, H., & DiTerlizzi, T. (2004). *The Spiderwick chronicles: The field guide.* New York: Simon & Schuster Children's Publishing.

Bloome, D. (1982). *School culture and the future of literacy.* Washington, DC: National Institute of Education.

Bloome, D., & Green, J. L. (1991). Educational contexts of literacy. *Annual Review of Applied Linguistics, 12,* 49–70.

Bruner, J. S. (1973). *Beyond the information given: Studies in the psychology of knowing* (1st ed.). New York: Norton.

Bruner, J. S. (1990). *Acts of meaning.* Cambridge, MA: Harvard University Press.

Carle, E. (1995). *Walter the baker.* New York: Simon & Schuster Books for Young Readers.

Cazden, C. B. (2001). *Classroom discourse: The language of teaching and learning* (2nd ed.). Portsmouth, NH: Heinemann.

Clay, M. M. (1979). *What did I write?* Auckland, NZ: Heinemann Educational Books.

Clay, M. M. (1982). *Observing young readers: Selected papers.* Portsmouth, NH: Heinemann.

Clay, M. M. (1991). *Becoming literate: The construction of inner control.* Portsmouth, NH: Heinemann.

Clay, M. M. (1998). *By different paths to common outcomes.* York, ME: Stenhouse.

Clay, M. M. (2000). *Running records for classroom teachers.* Portsmouth, NH: Heinemann.

Clay, M. M. (2001). *Change over time in children's literacy development.* Portsmouth, NH: Heinemann.

Cresp, G., & Cox, D. (2000). *The tale of Gilbert Alexander Pig.* New York: Barefoot Beginners.

Day, G. (2006). *Game day.* Parsippany, NJ: Celebration Press.

Dorn, L. J., & Soffos, C. (2001). *Scaffolding young writers: A writer's workshop approach.* Portland, ME: Stenhouse.

Dyson, A. H. (1981). *A case study examination of the role of oral language in the writing processes of kindergarteners.* Unpublished doctoral dissertation, University of Texas at Austin.

Dyson, A. H. (1993). *Social worlds of children learning to write in an urban primary school.* New York: Teachers College Press.

Egan-Robertson, A., & Bloome, D. (1998). *Students as researchers of culture and language in their own communities.* Cresskill, NJ: Hampton Press.

Elbaz, F. (1981). The teachers' "practical knowledge": Report of a case study. *Curriculum Inquiry, 11,* 43–71.

Freire, P., & Macedo, D. (1987). *Literacy: Reading the word and the world.* Boston: Bergin & Garvey.

Fritz, J., & Hyman, T. S. (1976). *Will you sign here, John Hancock?* New York: Coward, McCann & Geoghegan.

Gambrell, L. B., Morrow, L. M., & Pressley, M. (2007). *Best practices in literacy instruction* (3rd ed.). New York: Guilford Press.

Gee, J. P. (1989). What is literacy? *Journal of Education, 171*(1), 18–25.

Gee, J. P. (1999). *An introduction to discourse analysis: Theory and method.* New York: Routledge.

Gee, J. P. (2005). *Social linguistics and literacies: Ideology in discourses* (2nd ed.). New York: Falmer Press.

Geertz, C. (2000). *Local knowledge: Further essays in interpretive anthropology* (3rd ed.). New York: Basic Books.

Genishi, C. (1992). *Ways of assessing children and curriculum: Stories of early childhood practice.* New York: Teachers College Press.

Giblin, J., & Dooling, M. (1994). *Thomas Jefferson: A picture book biography.* New York: Scholastic.

Gilmore, P. (1986). Sub-rosa literacy: Peers, play, and ownership in literacy acquisition. In B. B. Schieffelin & P. Gilmore (Eds.), *The acquisition of literacy: Ethnographic perspectives*. Norwood, NJ: Ablex.

Goodman, K. S. (1968). *The psycholinguistic nature of the reading process*. Detroit: Wayne State University Press.

Goodman, K. S. (1969). Analysis of oral reading miscues: Applied psycholinguistics. *Reading Research Quarterly*, 5(1), 9–30.

Goodman, K. S. (1973). *Miscue analysis: Applications to reading instruction*. Urbana, IL: ERIC Clearinghouse on Reading and Communication Skills.

Goodman, K. S. (1979). The know-more and know-nothing movements in reading: A personal response. *Language Arts*, 56(6), 657–663.

Goodman, K. S. (1996). *On reading*. Portsmouth, NH: Heinemann.

Goodman, K. S., Goodman, Y. M., & Hood, W. J. (1989). *The whole language evaluation book*. Portsmouth, NH: Heinemann.

Green, J. L., & Wallat, C. (1981). *Ethnography and language in educational settings* (Vol. 5). Norwood, NJ: Ablex.

Gumperz, J. J., & Hymes, D. H. (1986). *Directions in sociolinguistics: The ethnography of communication*. New York: Blackwell.

International Reading Association. (2003). *Standards for reading professionals*. Newark, NJ: International Reading Association.

Keene, E., & Zimmerman, S. (2007). *Mosaic of thought: The power of comprehension strategy instruction* (2nd ed.). Portsmouth, NH: Heinemann.

Kellogg, S. (2002). *The three little pigs*. New York: Morrow Junior Books.

Konigsburg, E. L. (1998). *The view from Saturday* (limited teacher's ed.). New York: Aladdin Paperbacks.

Langer, J. A. (1987). *Language, literacy, and culture: Issues of society and schooling*. Norwood, NJ: Ablex.

Lankshear, C. (1997). *Changing literacies*. Philadelphia, PA: Open University Press.

Lave, J. (1993). *Understanding practice: Perspectives on activity and context*. Cambridge: Cambridge University Press.

Lyons, C. (2003). *Teaching struggling readers: How to use brain-based research to maximize learning*. Portsmouth, NH: Heinemann.

Lyons, C., & Pinnell, G. S. (2001). *Systems for change in literacy education: A guide to professional development*. Portsmouth, NH: Heinemann.

MacHale, D. J. (2003). *Pendragon: The lost city of Faar*. New York: Aladdin Paperbacks.

Marcus, G. E. (1998). *Ethnography through thick and thin*. Princeton, NJ: Princeton University Press.

Marshall, J. (1993). *Red riding hood*. New York: Penguin Books USA Inc.

Meier, D. (2002). *In schools we trust: Creating communities of learning in an era of testing and standardization*. Boston: Beacon Press.

Moll, L. C. (1990). *Vygotsky and education: Instructional implications and applications of sociohistorical psychology*. Cambridge: Cambridge University Press.

Morrow, L. M. (2003). *Organizing and managing the language arts block: A professional development guide*. New York: Guilford Press.

Morrow, L. M., Gambrell, L. B., & Pressley, M. (2003). *Best practices in literacy instruction* (2nd ed.). New York: Guilford Press.

Napoli, D. J., Kane, M., & Petrosino, T. (2001). *Rocky: The cat who barks*. New York: Dutton Children's Books.

National Council of Teachers of English. (2004). Framing statements on assessment. Retrieved July 25, 2007, from http://www.ncte.org/collections/assessment/resources/118875.htm

Pappas, C., Kiefer, B. Z., & Levstik, L. S. (1999). *An integrated language perspective in the elementary school: An action approach* (3rd ed.). New York: Longman.

Paratore, J. R., & McCormack, R. L. (2007). *Classroom literacy assessment: Making sense of what students know and do*. New York: Guilford Press.

Rey, M., & Shalleck, A. J. (1989). *Curious George goes to the dentist*. Boston: Houghton Mifflin.

Routman, R. (1996). *Literacy at the crossroads*. Portsmouth, NH: Heinemann.

Rowe, D. W. (1994). *Preschoolers as authors: Literacy learning in the social world of the classroom*. Cresskill, NJ: Hampton Press.

Schieffelin, B. B., & Gilmore, P. (1986). *The acquisition of literacy: Ethnographic perspectives*. Norwood, NJ: Ablex.

Scieszka, J., & Smith, L. (1999). *The true story of the 3 little pigs*. New York: Viking.

Sendak, M. (1963). *Where the wild things are*. New York: Harper & Row.

Snow, C. E., Science and Technology Policy Institute (Rand Corporation), & U.S. Office of Educational Research and Improvement. (2002). *Reading for understanding: Toward an R&D program in reading comprehension*. Santa Monica, CA: Rand.

Spindler, G. D. (1997). *Education and cultural process: Anthropological approaches* (3rd ed.). Prospect Heights, IL: Waveland Press.

Street, B. (1994). What is meant by local literacies? *Language and Education*, 8(1–2), 9–17.

Street, J., & Street, B. (1991). The schooling of literacy. In D. Barton & R. Ivanic (Eds.), *Writing in the community*. London: Sage.

Strickland, K., & Strickland, J. (2000). *Making assessment elementary*. Portsmouth, NH: Heinemann.

Taylor, D. (1983). *Family literacy: Young children learning to read and write*. Exeter, NH: Heinemann.

Taylor, D., Coughlin, D., & Marasco, J. (1997). *Teaching and advocacy*. York, ME: Stenhouse.

Tharp, R. G., & Gallimore, R. (1988). *Rousing minds to life: Teaching, learning, and schooling in social context*. New York: Cambridge University Press.

Tierney, R. J., & Readence, J. E. (2000). *Reading strategies and practices: A compendium* (5th ed.). Boston: Allyn & Bacon.

Tierney, R. J., & Rogers, T. (1986). Functional literacy in school settings. *Theory into Practice, 25*(2), 124–127.

Tuyay, S., Floriani, A., Yeager, B., Dixon, C., & Green, J. (1995). Constructing an integrated inquiry-oriented approach in classrooms: A cross case analysis of social, literate and academic practices. *Journal of Classroom Interaction, 19*(1).

Van Allsburg, C. (1984). *The mysteries of Harris Burdick*. Boston: Houghton Mifflin.

Van Allsburg, C. (1988). *Two bad ants*. Boston: Houghton Mifflin.

Viorst, J., & Cruz, R. (1987). *Alexander and the terrible, horrible, no good, very bad day* (2nd Aladdin Books ed.). New York: Aladdin Books.

Vygotsky, L. S., Rieber, R. W., & Carton, A. (1987). *The collected works of L. S. Vygotsky*. New York: Plenum Press.

Weaver, C. (2002). *Reading process and practice* (3rd ed.). Portsmouth, NH: Heinemann.

Wells, G., & Claxton, G. (2002). *Learning for life in the 21st century: Sociocultural perspectives on the future of education*. Oxford, UK: Blackwell.

Wertsch, J. V. (1985). *Vygotsky and the social formation of mind*. Cambridge, MA: Harvard University Press.

Whitelaw, N. (2006). *Dark dreams: The story of Stephen King*. Greensboro, NC: Morgan Reynolds Publishing.

Wolcott, H. F. (1999). *Ethnography: A way of seeing*. Blue Ridge Summit, PA: Rowan & Littlefield.

Wood, D. J. (1998). *How children think and learn: The social contexts of cognitive development* (2nd ed.). Oxford, UK: Blackwell.

Zano, G. B. (2006). *Green Freddie*. Parsippany, NJ: Celebration Press.

Zou, Y., & Trueba, E. T. (2002). *Ethnography and schools: Qualitative approaches to the study of education*. Lanham, MD: Rowman & Littlefield.